THE
BABYMOON
EXPERIENCE

THE BABYMOON EXPERIENCE

How to nurture yourself and your baby
through pregnancy and the early weeks

CAROLINE DEACON

piatkus

PIATKUS

First published in Great Britain in 2010 by Piatkus

A CIP catalogue record for this book
is available from the British Library.

ISBN 978-0-7499-4247-2

Designed by Paul Saunders and typeset in Minion by M Rules
Printed and bound in Great Britain by
MPG Books, Bodmin, Cornwall

Papers used by Piatkus are natural, renewable and
recyclable products sourced from well-managed forests and certified
in accordance with the rules of the Forest Stewardship Council.

Mixed Sources
Product group from well-managed
forests and other controlled sources
www.fsc.org Cert no. SGS-COC-004081
© 1996 Forest Stewardship Council
FSC

Piatkus
An imprint of
Little, Brown Book Group
100 Victoria Embankment
London EC4Y 0DY

An Hachette UK Company
www.hachette.co.uk

www.piatkus.co.uk

For Janet King, Cynthia Deacon and Marietta Wheaton,
my children's grannies: for being there, for knowing what a new
mum needs and for making my first few weeks as a new mum
far less scary than they might otherwise have been!

Contents

PART THREE

Welcome to Your Babymoon

PART FOUR

After the Babymoon

Foreword and acknowledgements

FIRSTLY, I HAVE SOME apologies to make. As a writer, I have taken some shortcuts. One of the main messages of this book is that you – the new mother – need to be nurtured, so that you, in turn, can nurture your baby. If you are extremely well organised, it may be possible for you and your baby to retreat into your babymoon space without another adult around. For the purposes of this book, however, I am assuming that you will have someone there to take care of you. I am also assuming that this person will be your partner and, to make my life as an author easier, I have also assumed that your partner is male! So I apologise to all those readers who are single parents or who have a female partner; I hope that notwithstanding these assumptions, you can enjoy the book and take from it what you need.

I also address you as a first-time mother throughout the book, but the babymoon experience is just as important – if not more so – for second-, third-, fourth-time mothers and beyond. Please forgive the lack of older children in the book – they are there in spirit! In addition, I have referred to your baby as 'he' and 'she' alternately, throughout the book.

There are many people to thank: Anne Lawrance at Piatkus, for her enthusiastic support and Joanna Devereux at Pollinger, for making it happen; Karen Sage and Elaine Antcliff, for their careful reading of sections of the manuscript and for their helpful suggestions and corrections; and an especially big thank you to Anne Newman for her diligent copy-editing.

Thanks, as always, to my family, for leaving me in peace when needed; thank you to all those parents who shared their intimate stories with me; and, finally, thanks to everyone out there who said, 'Yes, this book is just what women today need'. That kept me going!

Caroline Deacon, September 2009

The babymoon concept

So you're going to have a baby. Congratulations! From my own experience, as a mother of three and having worked with hundreds of mothers through my NCT (National Childbirth Trust) work, I do believe that nothing else that happens to you in your life will change your way of being more profoundly than becoming a mother. This is an awesome time for you – and I mean awesome in the literal sense, in that it will truly fill you with awe.

The problem – and the reason for this book – is that the society into which your baby will be born doesn't necessarily view this profound event in the same way.

Ever since we started competing for equal status with men in the workforce, there have been women who have given birth and appeared back at their desks within a few days. You can probably even name a few. And society seems to view these women as the modern-day equivalent of saints, regarding their behaviour as something to which we should all aspire, whereas what we should be doing is holding up our hands in horror and saying, 'For God's sake women, what are you doing?'

Becoming a Mother – Not Something For Your Spare Time

It's true to say that compared to our grandmothers and great-grandmothers, we do have it easy in some respects. We have washing machines and tumble driers, so we don't have to spend entire days just doing laundry. We have fridges and freezers, as well as supermarkets, so no need to spend all morning queuing in a dozen different shops, buying only what we are actually going to use that day. And we have clean central heating, so we don't need to be endlessly raking out fireplaces and dusting rooms full of soot.

But one thing that neither our grandmothers nor, in many cases, our mothers were expected to do was to work full time *and* raise a family. Running a home then was recognised as an important job in itself, whereas today, it has been marginalised as a subsidiary role, and so, by default, has parenting.

In previous generations, becoming a mother was less bewildering, in that girls grew up knowing what was involved, watching and helping their own mothers and being expected to take care of smaller children themselves. Nowadays, the new mother – who has quite possibly never experienced babies before and has probably never held one in her arms – is expected to know instinctively what to do: how to breastfeed, change a nappy, soothe her baby when he is distressed and so on, with perhaps one or two rushed visits from an overstretched midwife for support. There is no other job where this level of knowledge is expected without any prior training, and at a time when you are tired and your brain is fuddled from lack of sleep.

The good news is that given time, you *will* know what to do; in fact, you will become the one person in the world who understands your baby completely. And you will eventually bounce back into mainstream life too; it won't be the same life as before, but it will be something you can cope with and enjoy again. But this will not happen overnight.

The Babymoon – What It Is and Why You Need One

A babymoon is a period of time in which you allow yourself to recover, both physically and mentally, from childbirth. Although it is a natural event, even the most gentle birth with minimal intervention is arduous and will leave you feeling achy and tired for days afterwards. The energy levels needed for childbirth are equivalent to those required for running a marathon. Every woman needs time to recover from that. And that's without taking into consideration medical intervention or trauma, which are factors for many women.

Caesarean section rates are rising all over the developed world, comprising one third of all births in the USA, and with other nations not far behind. A C-section is major abdominal surgery, while other interventions may involve instrumental deliveries (forceps and/or ventouse) and episiotomies (cutting through the pelvic floor and subsequent stitching). Normally, anyone who has undergone major surgery is told to rest and take it easy for several weeks afterwards. People will gather round and look after them, nourish and support them. But this does not happen for new mothers, for whom normal business is expected to resume as soon as possible.

And a new mother needs time to recover mentally as well. She has been through a major event. Procedures – possibly invasive and traumatic – have been unfolding in an area of her body which, up until now, was private and associated with intimate pleasure. Even the most psychologically together woman needs some time to deal with this and to assimilate it into her life experience to date.

The babymoon is not a new idea, of course. It is a myth that women give birth in fields and then carry on with their daily work as if nothing had happened. Traditional societies have long known the importance of the babymoon period, and advice to new mothers in thirteenth-century Western societies was to spend the time in darkened rooms or specially created huts, where they were brought nourishing foods. Many cultures insist on a lying-in period of forty days, while for others it is at least three weeks, after which the mother is to resume only light duties, as and when she feels like it; in some cultures many women still return to their own childhood home to be looked after. Both mother and baby are sheltered in seclusion and visitors are discouraged. Indeed, in rural India the baby's arrival is not even announced until the forty-day period has ended.

And we too had similar ideas until fairly recently. Ask your grandmother; she should be able to tell you all about 'lying in', when women spent a minimum of two weeks in hospital after giving birth. And back in medieval times, a piece of white linen was tied around the door knocker to warn away visitors during the lying-in period.

Anthropologists describe important transitional periods in our lives as 'thresholds'; they can be anything from entering puberty to recovering from a death or birth or joining in marriage. Traditionally, we often coped with these thresholds by withdrawing from society and going into ritual seclusion; a period of mourning following the death of a loved one, for instance, would be marked by withdrawing from the world. Many such seclusions would last forty days (think of Jesus in the wilderness, for instance). How interesting then, that forty is the magic number when it comes to breastfeeding, in that it takes around forty days for your milk supply to become established, as we shall see later in the book.

Modern society has lost the sense of needing to mother new mothers, trivialising the entire birth event by expecting them to carry on as before, as quickly as possible. This seems to be high-lighted by the fact that if you do a web search on 'babymoon', you will find websites offering you holidays *before* the birth, as if pregnancy was the big deal, rather than the birth and its aftermath. Not surprising then, that 10 per cent of new mothers suffer from postnatal depression and many more feel they 'can't cope'.

So a babymoon is about recovering from childbirth. But it's

also a joyous time; a time to fall in love. In past times, when couples did not live together before marriage, the honeymoon was a time for them to get to know each other, to get used to being with one another every day, to work out how sex was going to be and so on. And even though people do tend to know their partners pretty well before marriage nowadays, they still expect to take a honeymoon. Why not then take time for a babymoon – to get to know and fall in love with this new little stranger in your life, how he is going to be, how your bodies are going to fit together for breastfeeding or for cuddles.

Your babymoon is also a time to come to terms with any mismatch between reality and fantasy. There may be complicated emotions to deal with; you may have been expecting a girl, but have given birth to a boy; you may have been expecting a large, bouncy baby and have a small, skinny one. Perhaps you were hoping for a natural birth and instead got every intervention known to modern medicine.

You may find that you are now more emotional about events in general; perhaps you cannot bear to watch the news, can't watch films where there is any sort of suffering or pain. You realise that you are no longer your own person, that now you have another human being dependent upon you. This can feel weird, especially if you were an unsentimental sort of person before!

While some women feel overwhelmed with love for the baby once she arrives, others feel slightly odd, as if this new person was some interloper, a stranger. Try not to beat yourself up if you are feeling slightly disconnected from this new person; you have years to get to know your baby and to fall in love! It will happen, given time.

Who Else Needs a Babymoon?

It's not just mothers who need a babymoon; the baby does too. While it is true that becoming a mother is a huge transition, becoming a person is an even bigger event. So far, your baby has had all his needs met. He has been held in a way that feels secure, has experienced a consistent temperature, has had food on tap, and enjoyed constant companionship – you. He's never been alone, hungry or frightened, nor has he ever not been held.

After birth, your baby will experience for the first time the sensations of breathing, digesting food and passing waste matter; he may feel too hot or too cold and he will, at times, feel uncomfortable or in pain. He will need time to adjust to this new world, and he will do so better if the one person he knows is constantly there, calm, relaxed and cuddled up with him. Generally speaking, he is going to take about six weeks to become used to these immense changes, so that he can be calm and then alert and interested, ready to interact with the world around him.

Your partner will also benefit from a babymoon. You giving birth may well evoke basic feelings in both of you, which go against any modern ideas of gender roles. No matter how equal you have been up to this point, things can feel different now. You may experience feelings of wanting to be nurtured and protected; this does not mean that you have suddenly become a Stepford Wife – it is a natural reaction to what your body has been through. And, after all, if you are being driven by instincts, why deny that this is happening to your partner too? Why deny any feelings he may have about wanting to protect you while worrying about bringing home the bacon? Don't berate yourself and think that all is lost. You can always renegotiate the division of labour later on, when you are back on your feet.

We have come a long way from traditional male/female, mother/father gender divisions, and we now expect men and women to play equally important parts in raising children. And so they can. However, having your partner sharing equally in childcare does not mean that he needs to replicate what you do. Your partner will be searching for a clearly defined role, and may feel worried about being excluded. There are hundreds of things he can do, but the most important one in the early weeks is to nourish you, so you can nourish your baby.

Which is where the babymoon comes in again. In 'nourishing' you, your partner is replacing those aunties, grannies and neighbours – all the women in traditional societies who took care of the new mother. This will fulfil his strong and powerful instinct to nurture and protect his family. He needs to bring you food and water, comfort you and shield you from the outside world. His job is to liaise with the outside world: to answer the phone, tell everyone about the new arrival, thank people for presents, limit visitors, politely ask them to leave when they have been there too long, register the birth and get the shopping in. He will also want to nurture the baby; to cuddle up with him, hold him skin to skin, bathe him, comfort him, rock him to sleep.

Your partner has a new role to adjust to, new expectations and new responsibilities. I suggest he takes as much time as he can (luckily, men are now able to take paternity leave after the birth) to recover from the birth experience, to establish a bond with his baby and to nurture his relationship with you, away from the pressures of the workplace. This will get things off on the best possible footing for all of you as a family.

Your Babymoon – Making it Happen

So while I am not suggesting that you take yourself off to a remote mud hut, cut off from the world, you should start by acknowledging that you – all of you – need time to adjust to the new life ahead and to get to know and fall in love with this new person. And this is where *The Babymoon Experience* will help.

First of all, in Part One, we will look at pregnancy as a time for preparation. In the same way that a bride gets ready for her wedding and honeymoon, we'll focus on getting into shape physically and mentally – luckily there are nine months in which to do this!

Then comes Part Two – the birth. Here, we try to think about making this as joyous an occasion as possible, minimising those medical interventions which make postnatal recovery that much harder and keeping you in control.

In Part Three we will look at the babymoon period beyond the birth in some detail. You will prepare your babymoon space, making sure everything is in place for this special time, so that you can get the most out of it once it's here. We'll talk about feeding your baby and taking care of both yourself and him in the very early days. We will also look at strategies to soothe your baby and help him adjust to the world.

And finally, in Part Four, we'll consider life, you and your baby in the immediate post-babymoon period.

Giving birth and becoming a family are life-changing events unlike any other you will ever experience. A babymoon is the perfect tool with which to enter this new way of being, and with this book to guide you, *your* babymoon will be a wonderful and memorable time.

PART ONE

Pregnancy: A Time to Prepare

The build-up to a wedding is a stressful time, but also a time in which to plan and prepare for this exciting event. Pregnancy is no different. And just as you want to look and feel your best on your wedding day, you will want to be in the best possible shape – both physically and mentally – for the birth and early weeks with your baby.

This part of the book looks at using your pregnancy time to get ready for the birth and babymoon. We'll think about how you can get in shape by exercising and eating well, how you can feel good through what you wear and how to get your head around the whole idea of becoming a mother; because even though you know in your heart that you are going to become a mum, there will be moments when it feels totally unreal, and often you will find it hard to imagine any of it. And not forgetting your partner, either: we'll look at ways of gradually getting through to him that he is going to be a dad.

Oh yes, and we'll be having a little think about some retail therapy too . . .

CHAPTER ONE

~

Yes, you are going to be a mother!

Every pregnancy is a unique experience. Some women sail through it, barely aware that they are pregnant, while for others, the discomfort starts almost at conception. How is it for you? Did you know the minute you were pregnant that this was *it*?

However it registered (or not) on your consciousness, your body will have been going through immense changes from the moment you conceived, and it is these changes which will impact on you, psychologically as well as physically.

Changes In Your Body – What to Expect

Your heart

To start with, you need extra blood to grow your baby, which has to be pumped round your body by your poor old heart. Pregnancy hormones increase your resting heart rate by about 10–15 beats per minute (bpm), so if your resting rate is normally 70 bpm, expect this to increase to 80–85 bpm. By the time you give birth your heart's output will have increased by about 40 per cent and the volume of your blood by nearly 50 per cent.

But what does all this mean? Well, obviously, your heart is working harder, and your veins have more to carry; but on top of this, your hormones affect the valves in your veins, allowing blood to pool, thus putting you at increased risk of varicose veins and haemorrhoids (piles). So try to avoid long periods standing still and whenever you sit down, put your feet up with your knees higher than your hips.

Fluid retention

There is also extra lymphatic fluid going to all your body tissues, so fluid retention can be a problem, making you feel bloated and uncomfortable. Again, resting with your feet up can help and, ironically, drinking plenty of water. Your body is more likely to retain water if it senses dehydration, so drink more if you seem to be bloated. You should also cut down on salt if you are retaining water.

Hormonal changes can also affect your teeth, making you more prone to gum disease, so make sure you visit your dentist regularly.

Your skin

Everyone dreads getting stretch marks, and there are hundreds of creams out there designed to feed into those fears; it really depends on how elastic your skin is, but most women do get them – it's just that pregnancy hormones make them appear darker than normal. They should fade gradually after the baby is born, but you can try to minimise them by avoiding putting on weight too quickly (see Chapter Three), as well as by rubbing vitamin E oil or cream into your skin to keep it supple. Concentrate on your belly, hip and thigh areas. Or you could try some of these essential aromatherapy oils which you can use in a base oil:

- ✿ Lavender or peppermint oil to soothe tired feet
- ✿ Lemon or orange oil to refresh
- ✿ Ylang ylang to relax

Sun beds are definitely out. Spray tan can sometimes look strange with pregnancy hormones, but pale English rose is quite a good look when you are pregnant, so don't despair. Make sure your face cream has at least factor 15 and top it up before you go out, because you are at greater risk of pigmentation when pregnant. Of course, this gives you a good excuse to splash out on an outrageous sun hat, which looks good with a chubby, pregnancy face (and yes, this will happen . . .) and big sunglasses will detract from any possible hamster look.

Also, be aware that your skin can become more sensitive during pregnancy, so you might need to change your washing powder to a milder one.

A salad for healthy skin

This salad should give you glowing skin and hopefully reduce your stretch marks, as it contains vitamins C and E, zinc and silica, all of which are essential for healthy skin.

Simply toss together washed watercress with thinly sliced cucumber. Peel and slice an avocado, and mix it in. Sprinkle sunflower seeds on top, olive oil and caraway seeds.

Your eyes

If you wear contact lenses, you should talk to your optician. Many women find them hard to wear during pregnancy, especially if their eyes are drier than normal. I found it impossible to wear contacts during my first pregnancy.

Your hair and nails . . .

For most women, pregnancy does wonders for the hair, making it thicker and glossier. You might be tempted to go for a huge change of style, but don't do anything too radical. Short styles need a lot of maintenance and don't necessarily look good on a chubby face. It might be best to chat to your hairdresser about a style that is easy to maintain, particularly after the birth, when you won't have much time to do it yourself, and when actually getting to the hairdresser with a baby is more of a challenge.

If you colour your hair, tell your hairdresser that you are pregnant and ask for natural vegetable dyes. Semi-permanents don't contain ammonia or peroxide, so should be OK, and highlights are not done next to the roots so, theoretically, they should not be absorbed into your bloodstream. Make sure the room where you're having it done is well ventilated though.

Pamper yourself with professional pedicures; you've got a great excuse as you'll find you can't easily reach your feet over your bump, and your feet do get a lot of hard wear with all that extra weight! Often, your fingernails become really strong at this time and grow quickly, but some women find theirs get brittle – either way, a good reason to take time out for a manicure!

. . . and feet!

Yes, even your feet might change size and/or shape. Mine got bigger and never went back; I have boxes of shoes I can no longer wear, so perhaps pregnancy is not the best time to be splashing out on new ones. Having said that, heels are much harder to walk in when your centre of gravity changes, so you might need to get some flats. If you are having a winter baby, get some chic, fur-lined boots for stomping around now and afterwards when you go for walks with the baby.

What to Wear

Many women look 'radiant' when pregnant because of the extra blood supply to the skin. However, the radiant look can quickly turn to hot and sweaty! And then hot flushes are another normal, yet annoying, part of pregnancy. Add to all this the fact that your waist is usually the first thing to disappear, and you could be tempted just to hide in frumpy tracksuit trousers. But don't succumb, as you will feel hideous.

What you need are layers, so you can strip off when you feel too hot. Stretchy cotton and jersey tops are great as wardrobe staples and you can wear these with long stretchy wrap-over cardis which finish below the bum (as *that's* only going to get bigger and wider). Basically, anything long and stretchy in a good fabric goes. You should still be able to wear your non-maternity jackets over the top for smartness (though probably unbuttoned).

Invest early in some well-cut, adjustable maternity trousers; not only will you need them for the pregnancy (and the next time, if there is one), but also for a few months after birth too. Jersey skirts or dresses (knee length or longer) work well with a wrap-over cardi too; wear with maternity support tights, which are an excellent investment. Dress everything up with your normal accessories – sparkly scarves, big bags, jewellery and so on (see Resources, p. 227). Soft boots look good with jersey skirts in winter.

Stopping your boobs from bouncing

It's difficult not to notice the waistband that's a bit snug, but it's easy to ignore the bra that doesn't fit any more. In fact, breasts are often the first area to expand in pregnancy and you may well need a new bra as soon as you are pregnant. Don't believe the old wives' tale that it's breastfeeding that makes your boobs sag – the damage has already been done in pregnancy. So minimise any changes by investing in some good bras early on.

The average woman (if there is such a person) gains about two cup sizes and expands across the chest at least 5cm (2in) during the nine months. Incidentally, your size doesn't say anything about your ability to breastfeed – nearly all women are physiologically capable of breastfeeding.

The first blow in terms of your boobs is that you'll have to do away with that wonderful invention, the underwire. Unfortunately, wires can press on developing milk ducts, blocking or damaging them. Even if you don't intend to breastfeed, you will still produce milk, so you must wait until it has stopped before you wear an underwired bra again.

If you're used to underwired bras, a bog-standard one probably will not feel anything like as supportive. A professional fitting helps. Nearly all of us underestimate our cup size and get away with it, but a cup that's too small won't offer adequate support. Breasts in pregnancy are heavy, and once the ligaments that support them are stretched you can never tighten them up again. Hence the saggy boobs.

Bra sizes

Bra sizes comprise two measurements: a cup size (where A is a small cup, H large), and a ribcage or chest size (where 32 is small, 40 large). If your breasts are large, you will need a bigger letter, but if your body is large, you will probably need a bigger number. As a general rule, cup size also increases with chest size. Thus, someone who measures a 36B will, in fact, have the same cup size (or 'volume') as a 34C or a 38A, the difference being in how loose the bra feels across the back.

It's important that your breasts shouldn't 'jig' up and down when you exercise during and after pregnancy. Tighten your bra straps, and watch yourself in a mirror to ensure they are adequately supported. Choose exercises that avoid straining your breast ligaments – cycling is probably better than jogging, for example. And you can even wear two bras at once for extra support, if necessary.

Top tips for a good fit

❀ Get yourself measured – a professional fitting could be a revelation! Otherwise, to do it yourself. You need one measurement around your ribcage just under your breasts. This is your chest size. Next, measure around your breasts loosely while wearing a bra. The difference between the two measurements will give you your cup size; roughly speaking 12.5cm (5in) is an A cup, and every extra 2.5cm thereafter increases the cup. Thus a 20cm (8in) difference means a D cup.

❀ If the cups feel baggy and it seems you are not filling them properly, undo your bra, lean forward and drop your breasts down into the cups. Then do it up again – this often takes up the slack.

❀ Your bra strap at the back should be low and level, not riding up, and normally the straps supporting the cups should be tightened slightly, so they are neither fully up nor down. They should be wide enough that they don't dig into your shoulders.

❀ A bra for pregnancy should give firm support and allow room for expansion, so it should initially fit on the tightest adjustment across the back.

❀ Extension straps, which clip on to your bra's own hooks and eyes can tide you over the last few weeks of pregnancy.

❀ Your bra might cut in under your breasts as your bump gets higher and higher. Try fastening the bottom hook on a slacker setting than the others, or leave it undone all together. Once the baby's head engages, it should get more comfortable.

Buying a bra for breastfeeding

There is no need to buy a nursing or feeding bra for general wear in pregnancy, nor do you have to buy a special feeding bra afterwards. But you should be able to free your breasts totally when feeding, which for a normal bra means taking it off – not always convenient! Feeding bras have special zip or drop-cup fastenings that allow you to undo one cup at a time, without undoing the bra. A badly fitting nursing bra can cause blocked ducts, mastitis and even abscesses, so getting the right size is vital:

- ❀ Don't buy a feeding bra any earlier than six weeks before your baby is due.
- ❀ If fitted while pregnant, your feeding bra should only just do up on the last hook, otherwise after the birth it will be too slack.
- ❀ Bear in mind that you will probably want to be able to undo it and do it up again discreetly, while balancing your baby on your knee, so during the fitting you could try undoing and redoing the different styles under a T-shirt, to give you an idea of how easy or difficult this is.

Antenatal Visits

So far we've only considered the more superficial changes to your body and how to look good in pregnancy; but what's happening on the inside?

No doubt you are looking forward to those antenatal appointments, so you can find out more about this and can have a friendly chat with a nice doctor or midwife who is just as excited as you are about this new arrival? Hmm . . . sorry to disappoint, but you may well find your antenatal appointments to be fairly rushed affairs with little scope for conversation.

Often, your antenatal appointment will comprise little more than a series of protocols (tests, scans at certain dates and so on) which, when midwives are very busy, can take the place of talking about how you are feeling or listening carefully to any concerns you might have. You may well feel a sense of 'magic' about all these protocols, as if, by relinquishing control of your body and your baby's wellbeing to the doctors, everything will be fine. But antenatal tests don't necessarily prevent anything from going wrong; they just provide extra information (which is not even always used or, in the case of false negatives, can start a cascade of interventions which are not always necessary – see p. 92).

Although these checks are meant with the best intentions, it is worth remembering that pregnancy is not an illness and you need to be involved in whatever is happening to your body. So if someone says or suggests something you are not sure about, ask for an explanation, and keep asking until you are either quite clear that you agree with them, or, if not, don't be afraid to say no.

A useful mnemonic to help you in your dealings with health professionals during pregnancy and labour is BRAIN:

✿ What are the Benefits of whatever you are suggesting?
✿ What are the Risks of what you are suggesting?
✿ What are the Alternatives?
✿ What does my Intuition tell me? (Very important this – don't disregard your own gut feeling. It is often right.)
✿ What happens if we do Nothing? (This is not as feeble as it sounds – sometimes waiting is the best option. For instance, if you are being offered an induction because you are overdue, sometimes waiting a day or two is all that it takes and you may go spontaneously into labour.)

Another thing about your antenatal care which can be disconcerting, is that you may meet different people every time, each of whom has a different take on things. When choosing your antenatal care, see if you can arrange for continuity of carers, i.e. to be seen throughout by one midwife, or one of a small team (see p. 128 to find out why knowing your midwife is important). That way, you can begin to develop a relationship and understand each other; there is less risk then that you will be given contradictory information and advice, and more possibility of sitting down and actually talking about the things that concern you as an individual.

But do remember that most well-nourished and healthy women in developed countries will have a safe pregnancy and birth. It is poverty which creates risk; in the Third World, perinatal mortality rates are more than ten times higher than anywhere in the First World.

A PARENT'S TIP

I used to go to the hairdresser every month before I became a mum. Afterwards, I realised that it was going to be impossible to drag my new baby along to the salon while I sat immobile in the chair! I wasn't keen on him inhaling all the fumes, either. Luckily, I found a great hairdresser who would come to my house. I thought it would only be a temporary measure, but then I realised toddlers and salons don't mix either, then there was another baby, then another, and before I knew it, eight years had passed. Eventually, she was cutting the whole family's hair and the cuttings were doing wonders for the compost heap!

Jane, mother of John (aged nine), Francis (eight) and Alexandra (five)

CHAPTER TWO

Eating for two?

Looking great and keeping your body toned and supple are important, but having a good diet is the most essential thing you can do for your growing baby. If you ate healthily before you became pregnant, you will already have set yourself up to cope with the extra strain of growing a baby, and perhaps to face the early days of morning sickness when eating may be the last thing on your mind. Healthy eating habits will also be so important when you reach your babymoon, when being well nourished is important in helping you to recover. During your babymoon, you won't feel like preparing elaborate meals, yet you will probably feel the need to snack a lot while breastfeeding. So if up till now you've subsisted on instant meals and takeaways, you need to change. Get into good eating habits and ensure there are no deficiencies lurking in your diet; this chapter will show you how.

Ideal Weight Gain in Pregnancy

It is an old wives' tale that you need to 'eat for two'; you don't have to eat much more than usual, but you shouldn't diet, and you must take care that your food contains enough nutrients to supply your baby without robbing yourself.

It is estimated that most women only need 200 extra calories a day, which is not a lot – say, a handful of apricots, a small yoghurt or a glass of Coke. Your recommended weight gain over the entire pregnancy will depend on your body mass index (BMI – an estimate of a healthy or 'ideal' body weight, based on height) at the start; if this was normal (around 20–25), you should aim to gain no more than 10–12.5kg in total. (It won't be all baby: don't forget there is also a placenta, amniotic fluid, as well as all that extra blood!) If your BMI is more than 26, aim to gain less weight, while ensuring that your diet is high quality, and if your BMI is under 20, aim to gain more.

Some women take pregnancy as an excuse to pig out: 'Oh well, I am eating for two, and I'll lose all the weight afterwards.' Wrong! Unfortunately, our bodies don't know that we have constant access to food; they are programmed to function as if we are still foraging for berries in the wilderness. So if you eat tons, your body will store all excess as fat in case of famine and will grimly hang on to it.

To avoid gaining weight too quickly, watch the size of your portions; this is easier than counting calories. As a rough measure, at a main meal, aim for a portion of protein and a portion of carbohydrate, each no bigger than your clenched fist or a quarter of your plate, then fill the other half of your plate with vegetables.

Your Baby: She Is What You Eat

What you actually eat – quality rather than quantity – is what you need to focus on. Malnourished women produce undernourished babies; and, worst of all, this programmes the baby's metabolism for life. Babies who are born underweight (less than 2.5kg) have an increased risk of illness and death in infancy, as well as a predisposition to conditions like hypertension, cardiovascular disease, respiratory disease and diabetes later in life.

So strive for a good balance, with plenty of variety. You should focus on fresh and wholemeal foods, organic where possible to avoid exposing your baby to pesticides. You need an abundant variety of fresh fruit and vegetables, raw or as lightly cooked as possible.

Protein

Pregnant women need to increase their intake of protein slightly; meat, fish, tofu, beans, dairy and eggs, nuts and seeds. Aim for low saturated fats; take the skin off poultry, choose low-fat dairy and limit beef and pork to once a week, trimming off the fat and grilling or roasting, rather than frying. Avoid bacon or ham which are high in saturated fats. A pregnancy diet high in saturated fats increases your baby's risk of developing heart disease later in life, but you can also actively lower the same risk by eating unsaturated and monounsaturated fats such as sunflower oil and olive oil instead of the saturated and trans fats in margarine and processed baked foods. And recent research suggests that a Mediterranean diet during pregnancy (olive oil, fruit, vegetables and fish) may protect your child against developing asthma and other allergies.

Nuts are a very good source of protein, unless you have a family history of peanut allergy, in which case you should avoid peanuts, but other nuts are fine. Beans or chickpeas, tofu and hummus are all good sources of vegetable protein, but you need to eat larger portions to get the same amount of protein as you would from animal sources.

Iron

You will also need more iron as your blood volume increases (see box, p. 25, for good sources). It is easier to absorb iron from meat than from vegetarian sources, but you can enhance the absorption of non-meat iron by combining it with vitamin C (found in most fruits) and avoiding eating phytates (cereals and pulses) and tannins (tea and coffee) at the same time. So for instance, a meal of lentils cooked in tomatoes or a chickpea and orange salad would work well.

Carbohydrates

If you have eaten a low-carb diet before, you need to rethink this, as your baby does need carbohydrates to grow. But choose complex carbohydrates – unrefined grains – as they break down more slowly in your body, avoiding sugar rushes, and the dietary fibre will help combat constipation. Babies exposed to the sugar rushes from refined carbs like white bread, cakes and so on, are more likely to be large at birth and are at greater risk of obesity later in life.

Snacks between meals

It's no good having healthy meals if you then snack on crisps and chocolate in between! It's best to acknowledge that you will need to snack between meals and be prepared with healthy alternatives.

Eat fresh fruit and raw vegetables between meals, with as much variety as possible in order to maximise your vitamin intake. For instance you could prepare a few carrot batons and celery sticks and steam some broccoli and carry these in a snack pot. Or munch on sprouted beans, which are easy to digest and good for you. Research suggests an apple a day can help prevent asthma in your baby. It's also a good idea to stock up on dried fruit and nut mixes, oatcakes and pots of yoghurt (ideally, natural).

Good eating habits at a glance

❀ Load your plate with fresh vegetables.
❀ Keep your portions of other food moderate.
❀ Go for healthy snacks between meals.
❀ Go for quality not quantity.

Liquids

During pregnancy, food will pass through your intestines more slowly to allow your body to absorb all the nutrients (isn't nature fantastic?), but this does mean you can get constipated, so keep your fibre levels up and drink plenty of water; this will also help control your weight gain.

Raspberry leaf tea is recommended as a tonic for the reproductive system, the idea being that it strengthens the muscles of the uterus. Don't take it until the final six weeks of pregnancy though, and stop if you find you are having lots of Braxton Hicks contractions (see p. 107).

If you can face it, you should probably avoid alcohol while pregnant. The problem is that we just don't know what is an 'acceptable' or 'safe' level during pregnancy and, for that reason, advice has varied over the years. At the time of writing, the National Institute for Clinical Health and Excellence (NICE) advises women to avoid alcohol altogether in the first three months of pregnancy because of the increased risk of miscarriage. After that, the NHS suggests no more than one to two units once or twice a week and that you do not get drunk. (**Note:** one unit is half a pint of ordinary-strength beer or lager or one small – 25ml – measure of spirits; a small glass – 125ml – of wine is actually one and a half units, so one large glass would take you over your weekly limit!)

Essentials for growing a baby

- ✿ Iron (see above): red meat, tinned oily fish (such as sardines), eggs, dried fruit, nuts, broccoli, dark leafy greens, fortified breakfast cereals.
- ✿ Folic acid (see box, p. 29): broccoli, Brussels sprouts, asparagus, peas, chickpeas, brown rice. Some breakfast cereals have folic acid added, but you can also buy folic acid supplements over the counter at chemists.
- ✿ Calcium: dairy products and fish with bones, like sardines, anchovies or whitebait. If you don't eat dairy, make sure you get calcium in other ways, for example by consuming soya milk or orange juice fortified with calcium.

Foods to avoid while pregnant

It is worth avoiding the following foods during pregnancy as they can cause problems either for you or your baby:

- Cut out soft cheeses made from unpasteurised milk, blue cheeses, pâtés and raw seafood, as they can contain the bacterium listeria, to which pregnant women are particularly susceptible. For the same reason, ensure ready-prepared foods are thoroughly reheated, and wash all salads, even those labelled prewashed.
- Toxoplasmosis can cause severe problems for your baby. To avoid exposure to this parasite, thoroughly cook all beef, pork and lamb till well done (i.e. there are no traces of pink), wash vegetables thoroughly and avoid handling cat litter trays. If you are gardening, wear gloves.
- Salmonella won't harm your baby directly, but it causes high fever, vomiting, diarrhoea and dehydration in you; not something you want when pregnant! Again, it's about avoiding unpasteurised dairy products, but in addition you should hard boil eggs and avoid uncooked eggs in icing or fresh mayonnaise.
- Caffeine can cause low birth weight or even miscarriage if taken in high doses (more than 300mg per day), so drink coffee, tea and cola in moderation (or switch to herbal or decaffeinated versions).
- Avoid liver or liver pâté as it contains too much vitamin A and can cause birth defects.
- UK government advice is to avoid peanuts in pregnancy, but the evidence provided by the Foods Standards Agency (FSA) suggests that peanut allergy is unlikely to be triggered in pregnancy, so the jury is out on this one at the time of writing.

Build-a-baby recipe

Take a bag of raw spinach, wash thoroughly, then drain. Peel and segment an orange, cut each segment in half and remove any pips. Stir orange pieces into the spinach, together with a handful of roasted cashew nuts. Drape some anchovies or sardines over the top and serve accompanied by your favourite salad dressing.

Eat fish — but what about pollutants?

Fish ought to be an essential part of your diet in pregnancy and also while breastfeeding, as it contains low-fat protein, as well as two important types of omega-3 polyunsaturated fatty acids, which not only lower your own risk of heart disease, but are also important for the development of your baby's brain. Research has found that women who eat fish during pregnancy are less likely to have a pre-term delivery or hypertension.

However, you do need to be careful which fish you eat, as some contain high levels of mercury or PCBs, both of which are harmful to your baby.

MERCURY

In the case of mercury, the problem is that the higher up in the food chain a fish is, the more methylmercury (a by-product of mercury) will be concentrated in its system. Your body does not recognise this compound as harmful, so it is absorbed by the gastrointestinal tract and, from there, is transported to your baby through the placenta.

The safest thing you can do is to eat fish lower down the food chain; so avoid fish such as shark, merlin and swordfish with their high levels of mercury and go easy on fresh tuna which has moderate levels. Most other fish should be fine (though best to avoid raw fish and shellfish while pregnant).

Incidentally, fish oil supplements are not necessarily free of contaminants either, although independent studies have not found significant levels of mercury in a selection of commercial supplements.

Vegetarians and those who want to avoid fish altogether should eat plant sources of omega-3 fatty acids, such as soybeans and walnuts. There are also prenatal vitamins with vegetarian sources of these beneficial omega-3 fatty acids and you can get eggs enriched with omega-3, which means that the hens have been fed flaxseed (linseed). You can get flaxseed yourself from health-food shops, but it needs to be ground for you to absorb it.

PCBs (POLYCHLORINATED BIPHENYLS)

PCBs are present in the environment due to the use of coolants and lubricants in electrical equipment, and even though production has ceased in the West, PCBs continue to be produced in other countries, and anyway they persist in the environment for a long time. We all have PCBs in our bodies, and our levels build up during our lifetime. However, they have more of an effect on a foetus, and babies born to women who have been exposed to high levels of PCBs are more likely to have neurological disorders and developmental delays.

It is hard to avoid PCBs altogether, but eating farmed salmon has become quite controversial, due to the discovery of high levels of PCBs in some stocks (one large study in 2004 found the levels of PCBs in farmed salmon to be almost eight times higher than in wild). So even though farmed salmon does have higher levels of omega-3s than wild salmon, it is probably better to stick to wild or organic during pregnancy, and also to avoid the skin, which is where PCBs accumulate.

Your Body's Requirements During Pregnancy

The first trimester

Early on in pregnancy, your heart rate and blood volume are increasing, which means you need extra iron. It's also important that your diet is rich in folic acid. The problem is that you might not feel like eating much due to morning sickness and general exhaustion. There is some evidence that pre-eclampsia may be caused by deficiencies in the diet, so you might want to consider taking vitamin supplements, at least for the first trimester.

The importance of folic acid

Your baby's nervous system develops first and it co-ordinates the development of all the other systems, but it is vulnerable; one in every thousand babies' neural tube fails to close leaving the spinal cord partly open – a condition known as spina bifida. The risk of this happening is reduced if you eat foods that are rich in folic acid. Even after the neural tube has closed it continues to develop, aided by a diet rich in omega-3 fatty acids.

If you are experiencing nausea or sickness try the following:

- Try eating little and often.
- Sip small amounts of water frequently.
- Some women manage bland foods like mashed potato.
- Avoid fatty foods.
- Try tea made from fresh mint leaves.
- Chamomile or ginger can help; try as teas or use root ginger in stir-fries or salad dressings. Ginger biscuits or crystallised ginger make nice snacks too.
- Cut out coffee and alcohol.
- Get more rest.
- Try acupressure wrist bands (sold for travel sickness).
- If you can't face the kitchen first thing in the morning, pack yourself a small breakfast the night before.

The second trimester

Hopefully, by now the sickness will have gone and you'll be feeling quite good, so concentrate on having lots of different tastes in your diet. Your amniotic fluid becomes flavoured with the foods you eat so that your baby can get used to foods she will experience when she joins the family. So the key to avoiding a fussy eater is variety during pregnancy and breastfeeding. Most women find this the easiest stage of pregnancy, but there are still a few things that can catch you out:

❁ Sluggish guts and clogged skin: if it feels like your system is generally sluggish, eat watermelon slices or celery; these can cleanse your gut and add fibre to your system.
❁ Cystitis: many women find they are susceptible to this. If you get it, drink a glass of water with ½ teaspoon of bicarbonate of soda. This neutralises the acid in urine, which is what causes the burning sensation. If you find you are prone to cystitis and urinary infections, take 100ml of cranberry juice twice a day as this has been found to make your urine more alkaline, thus helping to prevent recurrences.
❁ Vaginal infections: eat live yoghurt or take acidophilus; drink sage and peppermint tea. Add a slosh of cider vinegar to a bath or take a tablespoon of it in water with honey.
❁ Dizziness: the first step is to make sure you are hydrated, and the best indicator of this is your urine, which should be pale and non-smelly – if it is dark and smelly then you need to drink more water. However, you should consult your GP if dizziness persists.

Snacks in the second trimester

Now that your appetite has returned, you may want to snack more often than usual. Carry around with you a bag of dried fruit and nuts to snack on when you feel peckish. Walnuts are rich in omega-3 fatty acids and make a tasty snack. Dark chocolate chips can calm your cravings for chocolate and add antioxidants to your diet. Keep a full fruit bowl at home to graze from, and take a pot of fresh, raw vegetables in bite-size portions with you when you go out.

CRAVINGS

You have probably heard about women experiencing weird cravings for things like coal; I recently heard of someone who needed to lick the hubcaps of cars! Fortunately, however, the three most common pregnancy cravings are actually chocolate, salt and fresh fruit. Salt is OK in moderation; if you crave more than is sensible (bearing in mind that your maximum daily allowance is only one and a half teaspoons), talk to your midwife or doctor about alternatives.

If you are craving chocolate, go for good-quality dark chocolate (70 per cent cocoa or higher). With each of my three pregnancies, I had tremendous cravings for chocolate around the twentieth week. Each time, I found myself absolutely gorging on it for a solid day, then throwing up violently. After that I was fine and had no more cravings. Completely weird.

Coping with the third trimester

Nearly there! It used to be thought that you needed extra calcium at this stage, as your baby would draw what she needs from your reserves, leaving you vulnerable to osteoporosis later in life. However, newer research indicates that you actually absorb calcium more efficiently when you are pregnant, so as long as you maintain sensible levels, you should be fine. Dairy products are the most efficient source of calcium, but this does not mean you have to have a high-fat diet as you get just as much calcium from skimmed milk. You do need plenty of vitamin D for your body to absorb calcium, so this is a good excuse to lie around in the sun, if it's the right time of year, using sunscreen, of course. Otherwise, you can also get vitamin D from oily fish and eggs. (Incidentally, vitamin D is also important for children as it prevents rickets, which has been making a bit of a reappearance in the UK, blamed on our indoor lifestyles and paranoia about sunshine.)

At this stage in pregnancy, your baby's nervous system is undergoing a period of dramatic growth, so ensure you continue to get those omega-3 fatty acids. Most of the iron your baby needs is also taken up now, and this is a common time for pregnant women to get anaemia, so eat iron-rich foods, combined with vitamin C to maximise absorption. Be aware that being anaemic will make you feel run down, so you may well want to rest quite a bit.

Heartburn

If you are experiencing heartburn, the following may help:

- ✿ Eat little and often.
- ✿ Avoid fatty foods.
- ✿ Plain yoghurt at the end of a meal seems to help as it neutralises anything that might be refluxed.
- ✿ Try not to drink too much liquid *with* your meal, but drink between meals instead.
- ✿ Try to avoid spicy or acidic foods.
- ✿ Peppermint, fennel and chamomile teas can help.

Constipation

Ninety per cent of women develop constipation in the third trimester; the solution is to drink lots of water and eat fibre-rich food; this will also help you to avoid piles (haemorrhoids – varicose veins of the rectum). Try snacking on fresh or dried figs throughout the day and have prunes for breakfast: soak dried prunes overnight in some water or orange juice, then stir a large spoonful into plain yoghurt or skimmed milk and mix with a tablespoon of muesli (this can either be shop-bought or home-made using wholegrain cereals, nuts and ground flaxseed).

Shopping for Healthy Eating

Is all this advice overwhelming? Well, the best way to ensure that you eat healthily is to take some time at the beginning of the week to sit down and plan all your meals and snacks at once and write out a detailed shopping list; you can then even order it all online. Shopping once a week with a predefined list is cheaper too, as you tend to just buy what you need and are going to eat, rather than wandering around filling your trolley with impulse buys. If you schedule this planning time into your life, you will find that home cooking can be just as quick as heating up an instant meal or ordering a takeaway, as well as being far healthier and cheaper. When you have children you are going to want to rely on home cooking far more.

Pregnancy is a good time to rope your partner into doing the food shopping. Give him the list and get him to shop while you are there, so he is perfectly capable of doing it all on his own during the babymoon. Otherwise, you risk endless plaintive phone calls from the supermarket from him, asking which aisle the soup is in, just how many carrots you need and which brand of nappies to buy!

Incidentally, never shop on an empty stomach; if you do, you'll find the chocolate biscuits and high-carb meals calling out to you, 'Buy me, eat me . . .'

A PARENT'S TIP

During the last month of pregnancy with my first child Lewis, I had to avoid all spicy and rich foods as I had incredibly bad heartburn. Eating little and often, a bit like a baby, seemed to resolve this.

A favourite and quick lunch was toast with pesto, melted cheese and whatever veg I had to hand: tomatoes, peppers, etc. Later on, I found this an ideal snack for toddlers too.

Erin, mother of Lewis (aged ten) and Tegan (seven)

CHAPTER THREE

~

Keeping in shape

M ANY OF US POTTER ALONG with the occasional burst of
exercise and then decide we need to get fit when faced with
birth in less than nine months. The good news is that as a general
rule, you can continue to do any regular exercise that you're
already accustomed to and, indeed, it is never too late to start something new. After the birth, your body will feel physically depleted,
but the fitter you get yourself now, the quicker you will recover
afterwards, and the more you will be able to enjoy your babymoon. So if you are at all unsure about exercising now, check with
your midwife – she will probably be all for it.

Why Exercise?

Well, for a start, if you don't exercise during pregnancy, you are
more likely to give birth to a low-weight baby. But also, if nothing else, you need to get your tummy and pelvic floor (see p. 39)
in shape. Plus, when you exercise, endorphins are released, making
you feel good for some time afterwards.

Your arms will strengthen with lifting your baby and your
legs will tone up running around after a toddler, but tummies
and pelvic floors suffer most in pregnancy, and are the least easy
to get back into shape. And if you do gain weight and look

'curvy' afterwards, you'll feel great about it if you have a flat stomach.

Strengthening your stomach will also protect your back, and this is so important as from now on you are going to be heaving a dead weight around; OK he might start as a nice little seven-pound bundle of joy, but what about when he weighs twenty-seven pounds and wants 'a carry' and you're two miles from home? Or you are shopping and he won't stay in the pushchair? Your only option then is to load all the parcels in the buggy and carry him.

If you have never been able to find time for exercise before, it's probably going to be hard to create time now, so you could simply change your daily routine to incorporate some cardiovascular exercise (see below). For instance walk, cycle or jog to work and back, or if that is too far, get off the bus or train one stop early and walk from there. Get into the habit of taking stairs rather than the lift. Or take your iPod and go for a brisk walk around the block after dinner.

Taking Care of Your Body While Exercising

Before you go mad with press-ups though, you need to know about relaxin. This is a hormone you produce during pregnancy to allow your pelvis to expand on giving birth. Unfortunately, this hormone does not target specific areas, so all your joints, ligaments and connective tissue will be loosening up, which means you need to be more careful about exercising. So if you are already a gym freak and don't want to give it up, decrease the weights and increase the repetitions, and don't overdo the stretches. You also need to cut out any exercise which involves you lying on your back after sixteen weeks, as you risk restricting the blood supply to your baby.

Get a fitness expert to draw you up a low-impact programme taking into account your pregnancy; and if you attend exercise classes, let the instructors know and they will be able to advise as to which exercises should be modified or avoided.

Dressed for exercise success

To get the best out of your exercise sessions, wear the following:

- ❀ Trainers: essential, especially with the extra weight.
- ❀ A good supportive bra: I wore *two* bras when exercising (no one noticed or, if they did, they probably put it down to pregnancy brain!). See pp. 15–16 for more information.
- ❀ Full-length extra-strength leggings: these might not be high fashion, but a snug pair will support your bump.

Feel Good With Cardiovascular Exercise

If you don't already exercise, that's OK – you can still start up now! Cardiovascular exercise is not dangerous as it is low-impact, and it helps to carry oxygen around your body more efficiently, which is good for both you and your baby. Increased cardiovascular fitness will help your endurance during labour, as well as reducing the likelihood of pregnancy side effects such as cramps, varicose veins and high blood pressure. Regular cardiovascular exercise also helps you to sleep better and, perhaps surprisingly, to feel more alert.

Cardiovascular exercise includes walking briskly, gentle jogging, cycling and swimming. Start with about fifteen minutes, three times a week, increasing gradually to thirty-minute sessions four to five times per week. You should aim to raise your heart rate to no more than 140 bpm; this means working hard enough to be out of puff, but still able to talk.

Once you have passed the twenty-week mark it is not a good idea to continue jogging because of the impact on your joints. You might consider switching to power walking, walking uphill or swimming instead. If you have been running for a long time though and are reluctant to stop, consult your GP and see what he or she thinks.

Exercises for Pregnancy

Incorporate the following exercises into your daily routine:

- ❀ Pelvic tilts: on all fours, with knees slightly apart, hump your back like a cat, drawing your abdomen in. Now relax and let your back straighten out. (Don't arch it.) Pelvic tilting can help if you are suffering from back pain.
- ❀ Abdominal exercise: lying on your back, draw your tummy in towards your spine, hold for a few seconds and release. Later in pregnancy, do this lying on your side or propped up.
- ❀ Arm muscles: you might want to work these as they may not be getting as much exercise as your legs, and you will need strength there afterwards for lifting and carrying your baby. Stand straight with your tummy clenched and your knees slightly bent. Holding your arm by your side, slowly raise and lower a bag of sugar from your hip to your shoulder, keeping your elbow tucked in by your side in order to isolate your arm muscles. Repeat on the other side.

Birth ball

The huge inflatable balls you see people perched on in the gym are fabulous devices, not only for training the abdominal and back muscles, but also for use in pregnancy and birth. So this is one piece of kit worth buying. You can sit on it in front of the TV and exercise your stomach and back while taking in your favourite programmes. When you have lower-back pain in pregnancy, sitting on the ball and rocking your hips from side to side can ease it.

Optimal foetal positioning

The easiest way for your baby to pass through your pelvis is in the 'occiput anterior' position; this means head down, facing your back, with his back on one side (usually the left). Babies can be born from other presentations, but labour and birth are often longer and more painful as the baby tries to turn round, and because a larger diameter of his head will be exiting through the pelvic floor.

As your baby's back is heavier than his tummy, it will tend to go where gravity tells it to go. So if you spend long periods sitting back, perhaps on a sofa or car seat, your baby may gravitate towards the 'occiput posterior' position, in which his back is against your spine. Of course, he will move around many times during pregnancy, but towards the end, when there is less room to manoeuvre, you want to encourage him into the best possible position. Sitting on or leaning forward over your birth ball for prolonged periods should help to do this.

Food for exercise

If long walks are your thing, here are some great snacks to keep on you for instant energy:

- ✿ A slab of marzipan
- ✿ A banana
- ✿ A block of dried dates

Exercise Classes For Pregnant Women

There are many exercise classes designed specifically for pregnant women; you might like to join one, knowing that someone who specialises in pregnancy is looking out for you, as well as for the chance to network with other mums-to-be.

Aqua-aerobics

Aqua-aerobics (exercising in water) is an ideal form of exercise for pregnancy as your limbs are supported by the water.

Pilates

In order to get a flat tummy after pregnancy you need to work on the transverse abdominis muscles, and the best way to do this is through Pilates, with its emphasis on core strength, alignment and posture. The movements are slow, controlled and non-impact, so they don't stress your joints. The whole experience makes you aware of your body, while working your core muscles, postural muscles and pelvic floor.

Yoga

Yoga is a similar slow, non-impact form of exercise which is great for pregnancy. Some yoga teachers run classes especially for pregnant women, teaching gentle exercises to help you with relaxation and preparation for birth (see Resources, p. 228).

TOP TIPS FOR EXERCISING IN PREGNANCY

* ❀ Eat three to four hours before exercise, as well as immediately afterwards.
* ❀ Drink plenty of water while exercising.
* ❀ Listen to your body – if it doesn't like what you are doing, stop.
* ❀ Don't exercise on your back after sixteen weeks.
* ❀ Don't exercise if you have pain or spotting or lots of Braxton Hicks contractions.

Pelvic-floor Exercises

No doubt, you've already had people nagging you to 'take care of your pelvic floor' and perhaps, like me, you thought, why do I have to worry about this? Well, for a start, if you don't look after your pelvic floor, you will probably never be able to go trampolining again after giving birth without wetting yourself. OK, so perhaps this is no great loss as far as you are concerned, but what about not being able to jump at all? Or jog? Or even peeing yourself every time you sneeze? And your pelvic-floor muscles also contribute to sexual pleasure, particularly your partner's, and even though his sexual pleasure might be the last thing on your mind after birth, you may feel differently in time!

Of course, you might have the opposite problem – a very efficient pelvic floor – making it difficult for you to let go of these muscles during labour to allow your baby to be born, especially if you have done a lot of exercise. (Horse riding and gymnastics are particular culprits apparently, although I too found my pelvic-floor muscles to be a little too toned when it came to birthing my first baby; this was through years of ski racing.)

Either way, whether it is all hanging too loose or too tight, now is the time to develop awareness of your pelvic floor, and to learn how to tighten it as well as to let go.

❀ To work out where your pelvic-floor muscles actually are, try stopping the flow of urine mid-wee. (Don't do this too often though as retained urine can give you bladder infections.)

❀ Once you have got the feel of these muscles, practise tightening them as often as you can during the day. Eventually, you want to be able to tighten them without holding your breath or clenching other muscles like buttocks, thighs or tummy.

❀ Next, progress on to being able to let them relax. One way I found quite useful was to imagine that they were like the floors in a lift. Tighten them in once for the first floor, again for the second floor, then back out to reach the basement.

Perineal massage

While becoming more aware of your pelvic-floor muscles and how to contract them is going to make recovery from birth easier, being able to 'let go' of them during labour will help you birth your baby. Related to this is the need for your perineum to stretch to accommodate your baby, and research shows that perineal massage during the six weeks before birth can prevent tearing.

The best time to do this is after a warm bath when your tissues are more likely to be soft and supple, but the main thing is to do it regularly. Start by lubricating your thumb with some plain oil like olive or vitamin E oil and slip it inside your vagina, while massaging the outside of the perineum with oiled forefingers. Keeping your thumb inside, add your index finger and move towards your back passage, thus stretching the opening. Imagine you are stretching the corners of your mouth. Next, try sweeping gently from side to side in a semi-circle, pressing gently down at the same time. If this feels uncomfortable, take a deep breath in, then start the massage again as you breathe out, letting your muscles relax. Continue to just do the massage on the out breath, consciously relaxing as you do so.

You might find this awkward to do with a big bump in the way, so it can be something you get your partner to do. It's not a sexy thing though, as it should hurt rather than feel pleasurable! If it feels pleasurable, you are not doing it effectively.

Pre-birth Energy

As the birth approaches, despite tiredness from lack of sleep or anaemia, you may find you have a burst of energy, a desire to spring clean the house or to decorate everything. This is the nesting instinct, and is best fulfilled in a way that does not drain all your energy – you are going to need that for the labour. Instead, why not redirect your nesting instinct into ensuring that your babymoon space is all ready (see pp. 165–6)? Have you laid in all the food you want? And the treats? Is everyone else ready for that special time?

A parent's story

Speaking as someone who doesn't normally take an awful lot of exercise, it is odd that I got completely addicted to swimming during my second pregnancy.

I used to get quite bloated, and I found that if I went swimming, I could do a couple of lengths, then I would need to go for a pee, then get back in the pool, do another couple of lengths and get out for a pee again, and so on, until I felt clear again. After a couple of days, I would start to feel bloated again, so would go back for a swim to sort out my system.

Swimming just felt so good; it got me in touch with my endorphins, and I would feel weightless in the water. The only negative thing would be feeling so huge before I got in, and having the lifeguard say, 'I hope you're not going to give birth today!'

When I went into labour, I spent my time in water then too, and really got into the endorphin zone so quickly, everything went really well. I put it down to all that swimming!

Laura, mother of Robert (aged fourteen) and Daniel (ten)

CHAPTER FOUR

Chilling out

F OR MOST WOMEN TODAY, pregnancy is a frantic time with few opportunities to chill out. But preparing for parenthood is not just about getting the old bod in shape – it's also about getting your brain in gear, intellectually and emotionally.

In this chapter, we will look at some useful techniques to help you during pregnancy. Having these tools at your disposal will also be incredibly useful during your babymoon too, and practising them now means that they will be second nature when you actually need them. Use them to help you cope when you feel overwhelmed in those early weeks; indeed, if you can make these part of your daily life, they can sustain you in the years to come as a parent.

Stress in Pregnancy

Unfortunately, pregnancy can often be a time of great stress. For working mums, the run-up to going on maternity leave can mean being under pressure from work to 'just finish off this project before you go . . .' And many first-time mums feel anxious about the pregnancy and birth, while for existing mums, pregnancy can be stressful in terms of trying to cope with active toddlers while feeling tired and nauseous.

A little bit of stress is unlikely to harm your baby, but there is evidence that prolonged stress can have a detrimental effect. Stress hormones can restrict the blood flow to the placenta and can even encourage your body to produce prostaglandins, which are the substances you will secrete when you go into labour (this may be why high levels of stress have been linked to premature birth and low birth weight). One study has also found a link between high workplace stress and miscarriage, but generally the evidence here is not clear. If you feel that you are under undue stress at work, it is worth speaking to your human resources department. Perhaps you could change your hours or workload. If this is not possible, maybe you could think about starting your maternity leave sooner.

There have also been studies which have found that some babies who suffer from colic have mothers who had high levels of stress during pregnancy (caused by things like relationship problems or financial difficulties).

If your life feels very stressful and you are struggling to cope, you might want to talk things through with your midwife or GP. Sometimes this can really help to put things into perspective. But it will also really help if you can take time every day to do some of the relaxation exercises in this chapter.

Relaxation – What's the Point?

Relaxation is not 'doing nothing'; it is a conscious releasing of tension, both physical and mental. If you have never spent time consciously relaxing before, then pregnancy is definitely the time to learn, for several reasons.

Firstly, being able to relax physically during labour is incredibly important; it allows the contractions to be more effective, it lets your body produce pain-relieving endorphins and it will, in fact, make the contractions less painful. Our usual response to pain is to tense up and hold our breath (see the experiment on p. 50). Adrenaline flows round our body, diverting blood to our leg and arm muscles, in readiness for us to flee the perceived danger. But, of course, we can't flee from labour, and diverting blood from the uterus can endanger the baby. Plus, contractions will feel more painful because of the lack of oxygen (think of how your muscles feel when they cramp).

So it's important to know how to relax when it comes to labour. Don't leave it too late to try though – during labour is definitely *not* the time to learn how to do it! You need to practise techniques beforehand and find out which ones work for you.

Secondly, you can use relaxation techniques in the third trimester when you are finding it hard to sleep; often these will work when tossing and turning or counting sheep do not.

And finally – and most importantly – relaxation techniques will be really helpful during your babymoon, when you are learning new things, like breastfeeding or comforting a crying baby, for instance.

Create a Relaxing Environment

If you find a special place to go to when you want to relax, you can carry that place with you, metaphorically, when you give birth. It might be the same place you are going to use for your babymoon. It's all about 'nesting'.

Birds line their nests with moss and soft things, and in many cultures, mothers prepare a birthing house: a space that is built around the needs of the mother and baby. The Maoris traditionally called theirs the 'nesting' house, while in rural Asia they build theirs close to water, so the new mother can bathe after the birth.

Unfortunately, in the West, our birthing spaces have evolved out of the needs of hospitals which are designed for sick people. Concessions are being made to mothers in labour wards now, and birth environments are improving, but it is still unlikely to be your space.

But your place to relax can be visualised. If you find an open fire comforting, when you are in labour you can close your eyes and picture that fire, the warmth of the flames, etc. It's about building up associations. Do you remember somewhere that felt particularly safe when you were a child? Being tucked up in bed? Or perhaps somewhere you went when you wanted to be on your own – behind the sofa or a den in the garden? Picture yourself back there. Conjure that place up until the memory is vivid. You may end up embellishing it, so there are details which were not actually real at the time. It doesn't matter; what matters is that the place is vivid for you now.

Alternatively, you could create a new place: a beach in the warm sunshine, a forest dappled with sunlight or a flowery meadow. Experiment now with creating a safe mental space. Then, when you feel stressed or anxious, or when you are experiencing labour contractions, you can take yourself there.

Right now, you can also spend time with your baby this way. Put your hands on your belly and imagine you are stroking her. Imagine how she looks, how she feels at this moment. Send messages of love to your baby.

Your baby on the move

Of course when you relax, your baby will choose just this time to practise penalty shootouts! This is quite normal; you've probably already noticed that your baby starts moving whenever you stop. Babies love to be in motion; they love rocking, swaying, dancing, any rhythmic movement just does it for them. When you are rushing about, they get all the stimulation they want, but when you stop moving, the baby has to provide that for herself, so she kicks and wriggles to self-stimulate; but that's fine – she needs the exercise to develop strong limbs and muscles.

Relaxation Techniques

There are hundreds of different ways to relax, and whole books have been written about the topic. If you are going to attend yoga, Pilates or any private antenatal classes (see Chapter Eight), you will be taught to relax in a variety of ways. You can also buy CDs which run through relaxation techniques (see Resources, p. 228). Choose one with guided relaxation, rather than just a CD compilation of relaxing music, unless you are already confident that you can relax without help. You could also record yourself or your partner reading out the basic relaxation method below. Ensure that you speak really slowly and calmly, with long pauses between each instruction.

Basic relaxation method

Firstly, get yourself comfortable: lie on your back with a small towel or flat cushion under your head, your legs hip-width apart. (Later in pregnancy, lie on your left side with a pillow between your knees and another pillow behind your back to support you. Or choose a comfy chair, but ensure your head is supported and that your feet are placed on the floor.)

Record this next section to play back to yourself:

❀ Once you are comfortable, let your breathing settle down.
❀ Be aware of how you are breathing, focusing particularly on the out breath.
❀ As you relax, let air gently into your lungs. Let them fill, then breathe out slowly, releasing tension with that out breath.
❀ Close your eyes.
❀ Focus on each part of your body in turn, checking each limb for tension.
❀ Start with your arms. Slowly tense all the muscles in your arms, your hands, clench your fingers tightly into your palms. Stretch out your arms away from your body, feel them become rigid, like rods. Feel the tension, hold it . . . then relax, letting your

arms flop down. Feel your fingers unfurling. Notice how heavy your arms are now as they sink into the supporting surface.

✿ Now do the same for your legs. Tense your buttocks and the muscles in your legs. Point your toes and feet upwards as far as you can (do this, rather than stretching them away, to avoid cramp). Feel your legs lift away from the floor with the effort. Hold it . . . then relax; let go. Feel your legs sink into the floor. Your feet have become heavy, your buttocks have eased and feel soft.

✿ Now move your attention to your back. Lengthen your spine by curving your buttocks up slightly, holding and then releasing them. Gently draw your shoulder blades together, feel the gap between them reduce and notice your chest being lifted away from the supporting surface . . . then release; feel your back making contact again with the supporting surface.

✿ Next, focus on your neck. Lift your shoulders; hunch them up as if you want to touch your ears with them. Feel the tension in your lower neck . . . then relax, let your shoulders drop, then drop them some more to allow the tension to drain away completely.

✿ Finally, think about your head, that heavy object your body has to support all day. Press your head back against the supporting surface, really push . . . then relax and let go. Now raise your eyebrows as high as you can, hold . . . now release and feel the tension in your brow drain away. Now screw your eyes up. Notice the sensation . . . then let go. Bring your back teeth together firmly. Notice how this feels in your jaw. Hold . . . and relax, let your lower jaw drop down, let gravity pull it away and feel your lips parting slightly.

✿ Stay like this for a moment. Experience how heavy your limbs feel and how completely relaxed they are. Listen to your out breath, and consciously sigh it out through your mouth. Exhale fully.

✿ When you are ready, gradually bring yourself back to the world, open your eyes and focus on whatever is in your line of vision. Take some slow, refreshing breaths and, perhaps, gently stretch your arms out to energise yourself again.

The visualisation method for getting rid of tension

✿ Take deep breaths in through your nose and out through your mouth. Close your eyes and listen to your out breath. Make it as long and as slow as you can.

✿ Imagine that the air you are breathing out has a colour – a strong, deep colour. Take a few breaths and see that colour flowing out of your mouth.

✿ That deep, dark colour represents the stress you feel inside. Carry on breathing and imagining that colour; watching it being breathed out. Now, with each breath, imagine that you are breathing out a little of that stress, and as you do this, the colour gets lighter.

✿ Keep breathing out that stress and watch the colour fade to nothing. Experience yourself becoming more and more relaxed, less and less tense.

The ten-second relaxation method

We often hold stress in our jaws, neck, shoulders and back. See if you can tell where you hold your tension, then you can use this ultra-quick relaxation technique.

✿ Clench your teeth and hold; then let your jaw go and your mouth sag open slightly.

✿ Scrunch up your shoulders, then let them flop.

✿ Now breathe in deeply through your nose and exhale slowly and deeply through your mouth. Try to exhale all your breath for a count of twenty.

This technique is useful if you feel stressed when you're at work or in public places; you can also use it in labour between contractions.

Massage techniques

As well as taking time to practise relaxation, it is important that you get your partner to practise massage during pregnancy, so that you can discover now what will help soothe you later, during labour. Here are some suggestions for your partner, to get you both started, but there are no rules – just see what works for you.

❀ To begin with, make sure your hands are warm. Rub some oil between your palms, if using.

❀ Shoulder massage: do this from behind, with your thumbs in the dips on either side of her spine, move them in a circular motion over the shoulder blades.

❀ Move into back massage with slow sweeps with the palm of your hand down either side of her spine. One hand at a time is often good, with the other hand resting on the shoulder. Keep at least one hand in contact with her body at all times, and try to be slow and rhythmic about it.

❀ Try circling your thumbs, working upwards on either side of her spine.

❀ Foot massage: hold her foot on your lap and massage the soles of her feet with your thumbs.

Just chilling out

While practising relaxation in a structured way like this is really important, you can chill out by doing other things you enjoy. Unfortunately, saunas and Jacuzzis are out, but you can bob about in the swimming pool or sea, and with your bump you'll float more easily! Or just have a long, deep bath with some gorgeous smellies. And here are some other ideas for chilling out:

❀ Chat to a friend on the phone.
❀ Go for a girls' night out.
❀ Potter around in the garden.
❀ Get out into the countryside for a leisurely walk.

Breathing

There is no special way of breathing in order to give birth, though how you use your breath will affect you. Try to notice how your breathing is affected by different situations. For example, when you are tense or anxious, what happens to your breath? And when you are relaxed, how do you breathe?

In practising relaxation, try to breathe down into your pelvis, as if you are touching your baby with your breath, and when this becomes natural to you, it can become part of your repertoire for coping during labour. But if it turns out that you prefer to pant or breathe quickly and shallowly at the peak of the contractions, go with it. It will be what your body needs. Just remember to start the long, slow breathing after the contractions finish, to reoxygenate your body, and breathe out at the end of the contraction to breathe away any tension.

It used to be that women were told to hold their breath in

second stage, to help pushing. However, breath-holding is not helpful. Instead, drop your jaw, which can encourage your pelvic floor to open up. Breathe your baby out and only push when you can't resist it, in order to protect your perineum.

If the midwife asks you not to push, you can try breathing in short breaths in time to the mnemonic, 'I must not push' (i.e. short, short, short, then long breath out on 'puushhhh').

Sleep – the Ultimate Chill Out

Of course, a good night's sleep or a daytime doze is the ultimate downtime. So it seems incredibly unfair that just when your body could really do with a rest, your ability to sleep seems to have gone to pot.

There are a few basic things to consider. Firstly, is your mattress still supporting you? You are probably quite a bit heavier now than you were when you first bought your bed, and it may not be giving you what you need any more. If your mattress is too soft, it won't support your back; too hard and it won't give at the shoulders and hips, meaning your spine will sag. In any case, mattresses become less supportive over time; when *exactly* did you buy this bed? A good-quality mattress should last for up to ten years, but many of us hang on to them longer than that.

Before you rush out and buy a new one, though, read the section on where your baby is going to sleep (see pp. 64–5 and pp. 200–2) and be aware that your lovely new mattress might get drenched if your waters go in bed, so either invest in a waterproof cover as well or simply buy a memory foam mattress cover to tide you over the next few months, then invest in a new bed after the babymoon.

Another thing to consider is your position in bed – and not in a sexy way. If you were always one for sleeping on your back, you might find this becomes uncomfortable as your uterus grows; and as for sleeping face down – forget it! The only comfortable position is probably going to be on your side, and even that can suck. There are some great pregnancy support pillows on the market (see Resources, p. 228), which you can use afterwards, during your babymoon, when breastfeeding. It does mean you are going to be taking up a lot of room in the bed though, but hey ho – that's pregnancy!

A few drops of lavender oil on your pillow may help, though avoid getting this on the skin during pregnancy.

A relaxation technique for falling asleep

✿ First, focus on each limb and consciously tense and relax it. Start with your legs, your shins, your feet and toes, then your arms, hands and fingers, then work over your shoulders, back and bottom. End with your jaw, face and forehead. Take a few minutes to experience this relaxation, perhaps going back over each part of your body and ensuring it is relaxed.

✿ Spend a few moments concentrating on your breath, getting it to be deep and even.

✿ Then focus all your thoughts on the tip of your nose. Every time your thoughts start to wander off, bring your awareness back to the tip of your nose. Don't tell yourself off, just acknowledge that your thoughts were still racing, but gently brush them away by telling them, 'No, later, tomorrow; now I am just thinking about the tip of my nose.'

Of course, there is a biological reason for not being able to sleep in the third trimester of pregnancy as well as you normally do, apart from your baby trampolining on your bladder. What is happening is that your sleep cycle is changing to be in synch with a newborn baby's cycle. The reason for this is so that when you sleep together and breastfeed off and on throughout the night (which is what nature intended, whatever you might think about this arrangement!), you can do this without really being disturbed, as both you and your baby will wake up and doze off again, together (see Chapter Seventeen, for more on this).

Journalising

Relaxation helps you de-stress and allows your body to rest and recover. It is also good for the mind. Many people find their thinking processes become clearer with regular relaxation, and they become more aware of their thoughts and feelings. Another way to get in touch with your mental process is through journalising. Do you really know, right now, exactly how you feel about becoming a mum? Excited? Terrified? Not even thought about it? Think about it now. Write it down.

Keeping a journal

If you have never kept a journal before, this is an excellent time to start. You think you will remember all those significant moments for ever, but they do fade. Start by recording how you feel in pregnancy. For example, you could record the first time you feel the baby move:

❀ When did it happen and where were you?
❀ How did you feel?
❀ What are you looking forward to now?

You don't have to faithfully record what happens every day, like a traditional diary, as you are unlikely to keep that up, but do try to get in the habit of jotting a few things every day, perhaps in the five minutes after you get into bed.

Record the highs and the lows. Then, when your baby is born, keep the journal going. Write down how awful you feel after a night with no sleep, but also how wonderful you feel the first time your baby smiles at you. And one day, in the not too distant future, you can produce the journal and read out the really juicy bits to your baby's fiancé!

There are some beautiful books you can buy as journals. Choose one that you feel you could write in easily; for instance if you have large but messy writing you might like one with wide lines; or perhaps you would prefer blank pages where you can draw or create diagrams and mind maps. And do choose some lovely pens to write with while you are at it; ones that will really tempt you to write!

You can also use your journal to create images for thinking about birth that can help later. The terms you will hear are all very medical and can be quite disempowering: 'an untried pelvis' is not designed to fill you with confidence, so how about coming up with your own terminology when you hear anything negative? This may sound daft, but words can be empowering. Take 'breast is best', for example – that implies, doesn't it, that breastfeeding is some sort of super ideal, probably unobtainable, while formula is normal. But what happens if we say 'breast is normal'? Feminists knew the power of words and challenged them to the point now where people have to watch what they say, but this has not yet happened for birth, and doctors can refer to you as an 'elderly primigravida' without worrying about political correctness!

So when you are relaxing, or journalising, think about some empowering words. So rather than an 'untried pelvis', how about a 'brand new cradle', which is supporting your brand new baby?

Journalising exercise

Write down 'When I imagine my birth I see . . .' and just see what comes off your pen! You could also ask your partner to do the same.

Your journal can also be used to record those vivid pregnancy dreams. Don't worry – many women dream about being unfaithful or about their partner being unfaithful, as well as dreaming about the baby (both good and bad dreams). All that this means is that you are feeling anxious and apprehensive, and your subconscious is expressing this in your dreams.

Journalising can be really powerful and you may discover feelings you didn't know you had, so try to write when you are in a safe place, and if you feel upset or worried about what comes out, talk these feelings through with a trusted friend.

Mindfulness

Mindfulness, a way of being which is developed through meditation and yoga, may feel particularly appropriate for you to explore during pregnancy. At the time of writing, there are no mindfulness classes in the UK specifically for pregnant women (although they are becoming popular in the USA), but there are people teaching mindfulness to the general public (see Resources, p. 228).

Mindfulness teachers will help you turn towards your experience, to stay in the moment. This can give you resilience and help you cope with the challenges of pregnancy and birth. You unlearn control, and learn to accept.

As the baby grows inside you and then during birth, you may panic and feel out of control. But being mindful is about being aware of and in touch with what is happening, and of accepting what comes – an ideal way in which to approach labour, birth and your babymoon.

Getting in Touch With Your Baby

OK, so you know your baby is there; you have been aware of her ever since that first pregnancy test. Yet in some ways it still is a weird concept to get your head round – the idea that you are growing another person. Have you really thought about what this means? How do you imagine your baby is going to be? Do you have a mental picture of her? Perhaps when you are relaxing, ideas come to you, or perhaps the journal will bring clarity. But it is common for pregnant women to find it hard to see over the wall that is the birth and to imagine the days, weeks, months and even years beyond. However, the more prepared you are for life with your new baby, the less of a shock the transition will be, and perhaps too, the smaller the risk of postnatal depression, as you struggle to come to terms with a completely different reality.

Here are some suggestions for getting in touch with life beyond the birth:

❀ Research every type of antenatal class going and attend those that seem to suit you best (see Chapter Eight), making sure that they cover the postnatal period too.
❀ Go and visit friends with babies; cuddle the babies and offer to change their nappies. Watch them being breastfed, if your friend is cool about it.
❀ Lurk in parenting chat rooms. See what new parents talk about, what they are experiencing.
❀ Indulge in baby magazines; see what the common issues and concerns are. Discuss the 'hot topics' with your partner (see p. 77).
❀ Sit and talk to your bump, and encourage your partner to do the same. Play music to your baby (this may also give you an extra tool when it comes to soothing her during your baby-moon: see pp. 202–3).

And Indulge Yourself . . .

If you are planning some time off before baby is born (and if not, why not?), do some of the things now that you may not be able for the next ten years (only joking). Like . . . going to the cinema, spending hours at the hairdresser, wallowing in a long bath, reading a book or newspaper, having a lie-in, shopping in places with lots of breakables . . . And, while you are out and about, keep your eyes open for available resources in your community for after the baby is born. Is there a postnatal or breastfeeding drop-in centre or baby café? Which shops are good for prams, or have places where you can sit comfortably and breastfeed?

A parent's story

I had three miscarriages before my son was born, and in those tough years, I explored not only how to make my physical body more receptive to housing a new life, but also how to create an optimal emotional space. I thought of it as a spiritual pregnancy – taking care of myself as well as I would if I *were* pregnant. I quit my office job and started teaching dancing lessons six days a week . . . but no more than two classes a day, so that I had lots of time for myself. I spent the time between classes napping, and journalising, learning the words to songs I loved and doing only one thing at a time. I only spent time with people who fed me and left me feeling peaceful and joyful (this was difficult, because I really did temporarily cut a bunch of people out of my life – but I didn't need their negative energy). And so, by the time I became pregnant with my son, I was in the rhythm I needed.

Sue, mother of Zen (aged seven months)

CHAPTER FIVE

~

Practical preparation (or retail therapy to you and me!)

Iknow, it's tempting! all those shops just beckon, don't they? Wherever you look, there they are – adorable outfits, cute little shoes and socks, cuddly teddies and amazingly high-tech pushchairs and car seats. Then there is the whole idea of preparing the nursery – choosing furniture, bedding, wall coverings; it could be nine months of retail overload.

But for now, you need to put the credit cards away, sit down, and take a deep breath. Your baby will not need all this stuff the minute he puts in an appearance, or even during those babymoon weeks. I am not being a killjoy, it is just that having children is very, very expensive, and pregnancy is not the time to waste some of the endless pots of dosh you are going to be forking out over the years on a few fripperies which you will probably never use. And because you won't want to be rushing to the shops during your babymoon, we will look at the essentials you need to buy now, and things you can leave until after the babymoon is over.

Clothes – Cute Booties and Stuff

You will need something basic to put your baby in at first, but just get the minimum. Every visitor, every relative, every work colleague you have ever encountered (and some you have never even met!) will get you cute outfits, with matching shoes and socks, all for newborn, and your baby will only wear these for about ten minutes before he is in the next size. Even if you were to rotate outfits every hour, he would probably never get to wear it all.

For the babymoon, the ideal outfit for your baby is his birthday suit. Spending as much time in skin-to-skin contact is going to be what you want to do, and given that most of the time you are going to be in your jimjams, your baby won't need more than this either. The golden rule is to have your baby wear as much or as little as you are wearing; that way he won't get over-heated.

Believe it or not, baby nighties are ideal wear for the baby-moon. Firstly, you don't have to deal with hundreds of poppers when you need to change his nappy; you just lift up the skirt and there you go. Secondly, they are easy to pull on and off a less than co-operative baby. Yes, I know that a nightie might seem odd for a boy, but really, he won't get a complex, and no one is going to see, anyway. My first two babies were boys and they were both in nighties; they are now strapping teenagers who grunt and play horrible computer games like all other teenage boys. So if you really want to buy *something* for your baby to wear, invest in a couple of cute nighties (see Resources, p. 229).

And what about you?

Of course, the person who is really going to need the cute outfit for afterwards is you! So shop around now for some heavenly bed-clothes to wear during your babymoon: soft wraps or a snugly dressing gown, some cosy PJs or long nighties. Make sure they open at the front for breastfeeding, and that pyjama bottoms have high waists with drawstrings or loose elastic fasteners.

Nappies

Yep, you will need these at the beginning; lots of them. You won't *believe* how many. So pregnancy is a great time to consider which method you are going to use.

You basically have three choices: disposable nappies, reusable ('real') nappies that you buy and wash yourself, or reusable nappies supplied by a laundry service. Of course, you could go for terries – generations of mothers before us did, and they are cheap, fairly easy to use, and make great dusters when you have finished. However, they are quite bulky, so they don't fit as neatly into clothes, and can also be difficult to put on tightly enough when your baby's at the toddling stage, to avoid embarrassing loss of pants at crucial moments.

Do investigate whether you have a local nappy-laundering service. These are probably the least hassle overall, especially if your local authority limits how much waste they will take away (we found we needed an extra dustbin every week, just for our disposable nappies). And actually the cost of laundering is not too bad; they supply all the nappies, so if you want to compare costs, assume you will use at least six disposable nappies a day, minimum, which works out at more than one pack a week, and compare this cost to the weekly charge from the laundering service.

The other green option is buying and using real nappies. The problem here can be the initial outlay; you need enough for day-to-day use but as your baby grows, the size changes and so you need to reinvest. Of course, if you are going to have more than one baby, it will save you in the long run. But it is worth looking in car-boot sales, nearly-new sales and on eBay for a supply when you start out. Also, you will need to decide which system to go for; most real nappy companies are happy to send you free samples, so take advantage of this and see which ones suit you best, and ask around. Friends may even lend you theirs. My suggestion is to go for free samples and loans for the babymoon period, and once this is over, invest in the type you prefer.

Incidentally, while you are shopping for all of this, do invest in some muslin nappies, as they are fantastically useful. I had one permanently on my shoulder and it saved all my outfits from baby sick, which always appears when you least expect it. And afterwards they are great for polishing windows and buffing up the car (so I'm told . . .).

Essential Equipment

If you want to see why having a baby is like burning money, just look at the price labels on all the things you think you might want or need in the first year of your baby's life, add them all up and then consider what you will have to sacrifice to pay for it all. Then, read on for what you *really* need to buy!

Car seats

The most essential piece of equipment is a car seat, unless you intend to travel everywhere by bus, bike or on foot. In fact, if you give birth in a hospital, you will need a car seat to get your baby home afterwards, so you do need to splash out on that now. And getting a second-hand one is probably not a great idea, unless it is from someone you know and they can assure you that it has not been in an accident.

When you buy your car seat, get the shop to fit it in your car (most of the big stores will do this for you). You want one that will fit on the front seat as well as in the back because when you are driving on your own you will want the baby next to you (but only if you can disable the car's airbag). If you are a two-car family, check that the car seat will fit into both.

Some car seats come with bolt on wheels to turn it into a

pushchair (travel systems). This seems to make sense (although babies need different size car seats as they get older, so check yours will not become redundant too quickly); however, it's not good for your baby to spend too long with his hips held in a seated position, and my concern is that a car seat cum pushchair combination could be so convenient that your poor baby ends up spending hours strapped into one position, rather than lying flat.

Thinking about a new set of wheels

If your current mode of transport is a nifty two-seater, and you are reluctantly having to consider a change of car, my tip is to get one with seats that fold out of the boot for extra kids. You may not intend to have five children, but even if you only have one at the moment, there will be times, only a few years hence, when you are trying to fit your one child and all his mates in for school runs and you will be glad of the optional seats. And even if you end up with just two children, if they fight like mine did on every single car journey, being able to put them in separate areas of the car is a real godsend!

The people carriers with seven adult seats won't be necessary for at least ten years, and the lack of a proper boot in a these cars is a right pain, whereas cars with boots and occasional extra seats just seem more sensible. On that point, a big boot is really essential – you have *no idea* how much junk children need to take with them, even for a day out.

Sling

Another essential piece of equipment, but one that gets overlooked, is a sling. Your baby is going to want to spend a lot of time in your arms, being carried, rocked – basically, doing whatever you are doing. And you are going to occasionally want your hands free. The win-win compromise is a sling. Wearing your baby means you can get on with your life, your baby will be happy and you can even breastfeed on the move, if you so desire. But shop around for a good sling. You want one that will be comfortable to wear for several hours carrying 6kg or more. You want to be able to get it on and off yourself, with a sleeping baby in it, without dropping the baby on his head (not sure how to test this by the way; use your initiative or borrow someone else's baby!). You will probably need it to be washable and, as your baby gets older, it would be good if it were flexible enough to carry him so he can face outwards, as well as facing you (see Resources, p. 229).

Kitting Out the Nursery

You might be surprised that the only items under 'Essential Equipment' are a few nighties, some nappies, a car seat and a sling. What about a cot and general stuff for the nursery? Well, this raises the million-dollar question: where is the baby going to sleep?

The magazines all show nurseries decorated in pastels and full of lovely stuff – cots, changing tables, 'must-have' items and furniture in which to keep those 'must-haves' – the idea being the baby will spend all day resting peacefully in the pastel room, probably bored senseless by the muted colour scheme.

Well, babies are not like that; they want to be around people. They are happy to sleep anywhere, and they can't actually see pastel colours for several months. On top of that, the safest place for your baby to sleep for at least the first six months, is in the same room as you, if not the same bed.

So if you are really intent on buying a cot, the first thing to think about is, will it fit in your bedroom comfortably, so you are not stubbing your toes on it every time you walk in the room? And if it does, and you don't have a *huge* bedroom, you may well be buying a cot that will be too small. Newborn babies can measure anything up to around 60cm in length, and given that most Moses baskets are about 70cm, you can see how quickly your baby might outgrow it. My first baby lasted exactly two weeks in his before he complained about it being too small.

Some cots convert into junior beds later, which sounds ideal, but if you have more than one child, you may end up moving number one out of the cot and into a bed to free up the cot for number two, so it is only going to work as a long-term bed for the last baby. The other problem is that those cots tend to be pretty huge, so unlikely to fit in your bedroom for the first six months. Which brings you back to needing something else early on.

A really good system is the bedside cot, and if I were to have another baby, this is what I would get. It straps on to the side of your bed, and allows your baby to sleep alongside you, but not actually in the bed. It also makes feeding in the night almost as easy as having him in your own bed: no lifting in and out of a cot (not easy after a C-section), no need even to get out of bed, but you also are not stuck with the baby in the bed for the whole night if you don't want this. And they work as a standalone cot too (see Resources, p. 229).

If you know you are going to have your baby in your bed with you for some time, then perhaps there is no need to buy anything at all until later. If you don't yet know where your baby is going to end up (and believe me, even if you have firm ideas now, these may change once your baby is here and you know what he is like), then you could still wait till afterwards. So perhaps hold your horses on this until after the babymoon, at least.

And what about the rest of the nursery, I hear you wail, as you clutch those paint and material samples you'd set your heart on. Well, as your baby is going to be in your room with you, and not in his nursery for at least six months, you have plenty of time to organise this. And I suggest it is better to wait until you see what your baby is actually going to need, and what the practicalities of layout, etc. are. It really will all become *much* clearer when you have a real baby to put in it.

Reality versus fantasy

By way of an example of pregnancy idiocy, I bought a lovely wooden rocking chair for the nursery when I was pregnant for the first time. Sounds good? Well, it was actually a very bad idea. First of all, I discovered I felt really unstable trying to get in and out of it with a baby in my arms, and was in danger of catapulting said baby across the room when heaving my own bulk out of the wobbly chair. Secondly, as soon as baby started to crawl, the chair was a death trap; if he pulled himself up on it he was hurled backwards on to his head, and if he got too close when someone was sitting in it, his tiny fingers got squished under the rocker. Eventually, we dismantled it, and it is still sitting in the attic in pieces. If only I had waited until I had a real baby instead of a romantic fantasy one . . .

What might be handy right now is to have a spare bed in the room that is eventually going to be a nursery, for nights when your baby is fractious and you or your partner want to get some quality sleep. You'll also find it comes in handy towards the end of your pregnancy, when you are not sleeping well, needing to get up several times to go to the loo, or tossing and turning with cramps, backache, and generally feeling uncomfortable. This is when a spare bed somewhere is brilliant; no, not for you – for him. You need the space!

Some of those nursery 'must-haves'

Here are just some of the things you could be persuaded to pay good money for:

BABY BATH

This is a waste of time. Use a bowl of water to top and tail, then if he needs an all-over wash, you can use the sink, a bigger bowl or, best of all, get your partner to take him in the bath, or take him in yourself. Most babies love co-bathing, and it can be a really special time for you too. Don't get in the bath with your baby when you are on your own in the house though – you'll never get out unless you have abs of steel. Have the bathroom really warm and the bath temperature nicely warm for you but not really hot.

Changing station

This is really just a very expensive changing mat, which in itself is a good idea, but any plastic mat with a towel on top will do. The plastic mat is essential though, as wee will leak straight through a towel and on to the carpet. And you are much safer changing your baby on the floor than on a changing station, so that the first time he rolls off he doesn't plunge to the ground.

Oh, and while we are on the subject of changing nappies, you might be persuaded to buy an expensive nappy disposal unit. Why? What is wrong with a dustbin? That's where it is going to go eventually, unless you are using washables, in which case, just get a bucket to soak them in.

Baby monitor

Do you live in a palace? Well, unless you do, you will probably be able to hear your baby cry, without electronic bugging devices. In the night, he is going to be in your room, so monitors are really only useful for when he is having a kip and you want to go off down the garden or wherever. We bought ours for a weekend in a hotel and took it into the restaurant, only to find that other people had the same monitor and we were listening to their babies and they were listening to ours! But it seemed like a good idea at the time!

If you are determined to get one, a simple listening device is all you need; breathing monitors and flashing lights are not necessary. Really. Oh, and if your baby won't settle in the evenings unless you are there, try setting it the other way round, so *he* can hear you chatting or watching TV rather than *you* listening to him breathing in a silent room. And beware: do not have a conversation about how awful your mother-in-law is and how you wish she would bugger off back home, *anywhere* within a hundred yards of a monitor, because when you come back to the sitting room, you will find her sitting there, red-faced and furious, ready to cut you out of her will for ever.

BOTTLES, STERILISERS AND MORE

Believe it or not, you don't need any of this, unless you are intending to formula-feed from the start. If and when you get around to expressing breast milk for an evening out (hah!), that will be the time to buy all this. But you may well still need it less than you'd think. My first baby had bottles when I was in hospital for a week and he was fed expressed breast milk; my second and third babies never had a bottle at all. At six months, they went on to solid foods and started drinking water or juice from a training cup, then a normal cup. And I never had to sterilise anything for them either; after six months they put everything in their mouths anyway, so were getting a healthy load of germs, and as food itself is not sterile, there did not seem any point in sterilising their eating utensils. And yes, I did have evenings out; I would breastfeed before I went, and again when I got back, and that all worked fine.

THERMOMETERS

You may become obsessed with temperature – the room's, the bath's and, indeed, your baby's.

Unfortunately, babies are not very co-operative when it comes to sticking a mercury thermometer under their tongues. If your baby is running a temperature, he will feel hot and will probably be miserable; and then you will ring the doctor, who will take his temperature. But if you do want peace of mind, invest in a special ear thermometer. At least then you will know whether or not to call the GP in a panic. You might also want to do a mini first-aid course if you have not done this before. It will mean that you know what to do in an emergency (see Resources, p. 229).

When it comes to bath and room temperatures, you can use common sense. Check the bath yourself by immersing your whole forearm, rather than just your hand which might be less sensitive to hot temperatures. Does it feel too hot (or too cold) for you? Then probably your baby won't like it either. Keep the room at a sensible temperature and dress your baby in a similar number of layers to you.

Out and About With Your Baby

Changing bag

You will have one of these over your shoulder for the next few years, so accessorise it with what *you* wear, not with the baby's clothes. I had a really hideous lurid green and blue striped plastic one, and I was so sick of the sight of it after three babies, having carried it around everywhere for six years!

There are some really gorgeous ones out there (see Resources, p. 229), but before you buy anything too outrageous or girly, remember that your partner will need to carry it too . . .

Here are some things to think about:

❀ It should look good, so both you and your partner are happy to carry it.
❀ It must have a detachable changing mat, as these are hard to track down when you are out and about.
❀ Lots of pockets and compartments are good, to carry spare clothes, as well as allowing you to keep clean and dirty nappies separately, for example.
❀ Straps that fit across your pushchair are handy, so you don't have to carry it the whole time; failing that, it should be not so bulky that it won't fit under the pram if necessary.

Prams/pushchairs

As I said before, one of the best investments you can make is a really good sling. You may find that you want to use your sling, not only round the house, but also when you are out and about. For instance, wouldn't it be easier to wear your baby in his sling when food shopping, rather than sticking the car seat in the trolley?

However, there are going to be occasions when you want to have your baby in a pram or pushchair when you are out and about. Prams have their uses, but unless you want your attic full of several different types, try to get one that will do everything:

- ✿ A pram which is also a car seat might suit you.
- ✿ Having said that, see if you can get one which gives you the option of allowing baby to lie flat now, but sit up later. It is also best if he can face you when he is young, but face outwards when he is much older. Not all combination car seat systems provide this option, however.
- ✿ It is good to have lots of room to accommodate shopping, as well as all the baby paraphernalia, but it needs to be sturdy enough that it doesn't tip over from all the weight when your toddler leaps out.
- ✿ Get adjustable handles, so your partner has no excuse for not pushing it.
- ✿ Ask yourself how much room will it take up in the boot of your car? (If it doubles as a car seat that will help.)
- ✿ How manoeuvrable is it? If it has fixed front wheels, it will be like trying to steer an oil tanker if you want to change direction.
- ✿ Get a big coverall for rain and make sure it fits your pram exactly. A sun shade is a waste of time though – as soon as you go round a corner your baby will get the sun in his eyes. Get him a nice sun hat instead.

✿ Make sure you can fit a buggy board on to it if you plan to have more than one child. They are excellent devices and the inventor deserves to be a millionaire, if he is not already one. No matter how good your toddler is at walking, you will need a buggy board on occasions, as otherwise you end up carrying a toddler under one arm and pushing the pram with the other – not a good look.

And While You're Out Shopping . . .

. . . you're not going to want to be rushing off to the supermarket during your babymoon, so stock up now on essentials: fill the freezer with nutritious soups and ready meals, frozen fruit and vegetables. (And think about setting up an online food shopping account too, if you don't have one.)

Here are some ideas for some easy-to-prepare, nutritious snacks and meals to have at the ready:

✿ Snacks: bananas; sardines or Marmite on wholemeal toast; bean sprout salad with raw spinach and a hard-boiled egg, all washed down with fresh orange juice or a smoothie.
✿ Main meals: lightly poached fish with couscous is easily digestible and good for you.
✿ Frozen berries are a good stand-by to keep in the freezer: stir into yoghurt for a healthy snack or liquidise for a smoothie.
✿ Mixed frozen vegetables can be stirred into tinned soup.

Baby Shower – A Recipe for Avoiding an Overstretched Wallet

A tradition from the USA, but one which seems to be catching on elsewhere, is to have a 'baby shower'. This is a celebratory party, held in late pregnancy, where your friends 'shower' you with gifts for the new baby. While some people will go ahead and buy whatever they think you will like, here are some suggestions you can give to friends and relatives if they do ask what you really need:

- ❀ A promise to babysit in six months' time (an ideal gift from a friend who is strapped for cash or for a teenager).
- ❀ Lots of food goodies to put in the freezer for later, either home-made or bought.
- ❀ A session in the beauty salon.
- ❀ Luxury travel toiletries to take into hospital or to use during your babymoon.
- ❀ Champagne.
- ❀ A subscription to your local nappy-laundering service.
- ❀ Set of antenatal classes.
- ❀ Promise of ironing.
- ❀ Paying for a cleaner during your babymoon.

PARENT'S TIP

I bought practically nothing before the first baby – mainly because I am so disorganised, I never got around to it; but, in addition, my sister had had a baby six months before, so she passed a lot of stuff on to me. The only thing I bought was a car seat.

I then discovered that people absolutely shower you with things; I got presents from distant friends of my parents who I hardly knew, and work colleagues bought me a baby listener.

The thing I know now is that you just won't know what you need until your baby arrives. I have friends who spent hundreds of pounds on stuff like pushchairs, which did not fit in their boots, or equipment they didn't need, due to their lifestyles. Your baby won't notice if he has second-hand stuff, and he will survive perfectly well for the first few weeks until you work out what you need.

I gave everything back to my sister when she had her second baby, and we kept swapping until we stopped having babies – it all worked out really well.

Catherine, mother of Siobhan (aged sixteen), Ruth (thirteen), Michael (eleven) and Daniel (eight)

CHAPTER SIX

Preparing to become a family

I T MIGHT NOT SEEM like it right now, but your partner will go through huge changes as well; he's just a bit out of synch, trailing behind you by about nine months. So while you are acutely conscious of being pregnant, he is able to go off to work and forget about it for long periods of time. You can shove all the cute baby pictures under his nose that you like, but it won't really impact on him in any big way until just before, or even during, the birth. You might not like it, but that's life, and he is not being difficult; he is just being a male. After all, to be fair, he doesn't have the sickness, heartburn or kicking to constantly remind him of what's to come.

So for your partner, life continues as before, and you are still the sexy woman he fell in love with, even if you feel like death most of the day. However unjust it may seem, you both need to do your part in keeping that relationship going if you want your baby to be born into a conventional two-parent family.

Fatherhood – Getting His Brain in Gear

There are a few things you do need to do to start tuning your partner's brain into Daddy mode. Firstly, make sure he comes to every scan with you. Seeing is believing. And, on a more sober note, the scans are there not just to entertain and enthral parents-to-be, but also to highlight any possible problems, so you'll want someone there who is going to be supportive, if there is bad news of any kind.

Incidentally, just so you don't spend the time feeling self-conscious when you go for your scan and end up missing the joys of seeing your new baby, wear nice knickers and get your bikini line done before you go! Oh, and take cash for the photo; the NHS still doesn't accept credit cards. Some places even do videos now and you will want everything that's going – probably copies for all the doting grandparents too.

Get your partner involved in some of the relaxation and visualisation exercises we looked at in Chapter Four, and ensure, when you book antenatal classes, that they welcome fathers-to-be with open arms (otherwise, avoid them like the plague or see them as an additional resource, not your sole preparation). We will look at this more in Chapter Eight, but for now, be assured that if you want him to start thinking about parenthood, he needs to attend the classes as an active participant.

Last-minute Holidays

Many people think that a babymoon is a holiday you take *before* the baby is born, and of course, going on holiday together, that last fling, *is* an important part of preparing for becoming a family, and may give you some much needed time alone to talk about the forthcoming events. But if a holiday is to be useful to you, it needs to leave you relaxed, refreshed and revitalised, so think about it carefully.

Firstly, it is probably not a great idea to book something too far in advance; how you feel now and how you will feel then could be very different. You might feel too uncomfortable to enjoy whatever you have planned, you might be too tired or you might even be unable to travel for medical reasons.

The best time to go on a pre-baby holiday is probably during your second trimester, when you are (hopefully) over the morning sickness and fatigue, but not yet too big or uncomfortable to enjoy it.

If your holiday involves a flight, check the airline's policy on flying when pregnant, and remember that any limitations apply to the way *back* as well. Airlines can turn you away at the gate even after accepting a booking, so you should get a letter from your doctor certifying that you are indeed as pregnant as you say you are, and that he or she is happy for you to fly.

But be realistic about flying. It can feel cramped and uncomfortable at the best of times; how will it feel when you are pregnant? There is also a slightly increased risk of deep-vein thrombosis, so wear support socks or stockings and put them on before you get out of bed the day you are going to fly.

Think too about the destination, in case there is a medical emergency when you are away. Will your travel insurance cover this? How will you feel about having a premature baby while on safari or on a beach in the Far East? The solution is probably to not travel too far, to pay extra for bigger seats or think about travelling on Eurostar instead, as on a train you can get up and move around more easily, use the toilet when you need to and so on.

Unless your heart is really set on going abroad, why not plan something closer to home? A mini hotel break in a city you've always fancied visiting or perhaps a spa weekend in a hotel near your home? Luxury hotels often offer short break packages, particularly if you are going off season (see Resources, p. 229).

Make sure you drink lots of water while travelling or when out and about sightseeing, and have a selection of comfortable shoes for walking, as your feet will swell. Keep the itinerary modest and factor in lots of rest breaks.

Of course, you don't have to travel to take a holiday. Why not just bunk down at home? Tell everyone you are going away, take time off work and hide away together in your own space. You could venture out to visit some local sights that you've never got around to seeing or, if you don't feel up to it, or if the weather is unkind, simply stay put and watch those DVD box sets you haven't got around to watching yet.

Hot topics for expectant parents

Try to use the time on holiday to talk about the future; to begin the process of joint negotiation over parenting issues. Some of the hot topics you might want to think about together are:

- Who sleeps where? Do you both think that your baby should share your bed with you until she is old enough to bring her boyfriend home, or does she only get access over your dead bodies?
- How important is it to each of you that your baby is breastfed?
- How do you feel about dummies versus possible thumb sucking?
- Childcare. Who do you want to leave your baby with if and when you return to work? What would be important?
- Schooling. How do you feel about education? Home schooling? Boarding school as soon as she can walk?
- Finances. How will you spend your money now that there might be less of it *and* it has to go further?
- Discipline. What are your feelings about rules and regulations for your children? Spare the rod and spoil the child? Or anything goes? (It is worth talking now about how to present a 'united front'; it's important that you don't contradict each other in front of the children.)
- Holidays, Christmas, etc. – where are you going to spend them now that you are a family?
- How do you feel about family meals, table manners, that sort of thing? (My suggestion is that you always sit down and eat one meal together every day. Now that our kids are teenagers I am so pleased that we got into this habit, as this is the one time of the day when we all communicate.)

The Modern Father

Becoming a father today is more difficult, but arguably more rewarding, than at any time before. Up until fairly recently, what men and women each brought to parenthood was quite clearly defined, and that division of labour reflected the needs of the economic workplace, or perhaps you could say the workplace reflected that division of labour in the home. In any case, Dad was there to bring home the bacon and perhaps provide a bit of discipline when asked, but that was as far as his involvement went, in the early days, at least. When kids got bigger, Dad was there for initiation into the outside world; showing sons how to do manly stuff, vetting daughters' boyfriends, chopping wood, changing light bulbs, you know the sort of thing. There was none of this attending birth and helping in the early days – that was definitely 'women's work'.

Nowadays, however, most fathers attend the birth of their children, most help in the period after the birth and most get up to help with the baby at night. Oh yes, and they expect women to change light bulbs too.

In addition, it is common for both partners to work, and it is generally expected that they both continue to work after becoming parents. Of course, there are still assumptions that the early days are the woman's responsibility, and this is reflected in the difference in length of maternity and paternity leave, but nevertheless, given that women are expected to return to work, they in turn expect their partners to be more equitably involved in bringing up the children. Interestingly too, a study of ninety non-industrial societies found that the more men were involved in child rearing, the higher the status of women in that society.

Families – In All Their Guises

The other big change in our society is about how that relationship, which produced the baby in the first place, actually progresses.

Up until about the 1970s, there was a very traditional pattern to becoming a family. First, there would be a period of courtship, which may have taken some time, followed by engagement, marriage, then babies, in that order. Usually too, at this point, the woman, if she was from a middle-class background, would stop working and stay at home full-time to bring up the children, while working-class women would change their working patterns and be expected to be primarily a homemaker, even if she had to work outside the home to bring in extra cash. Of course, not all families evolved like this, but there was a stigma attached to having a baby outside this structure, and many babies born 'outside wedlock' were put up for adoption until the changes in thinking brought about by the feminist movement in the 1970s. Certainly, couples got married as quickly as possible if they discovered a baby was on its way.

Things have changed enormously since then. Nowadays, only 60 per cent of people are married when they become parents,

25 per cent are cohabiting and the other 15 per cent are a disparate group, some of whom are separated or divorced, some who are closely involved and others who are 'just friends'.

While 18–30 per cent of couples feel their relationship improves after having a baby, for most of us, becoming parents puts a large strain on things. The problem is that if a couple are still getting to know each other, or are not particularly committed before they have a baby, they are less likely to be together a year after the baby is born. (Ninety-four per cent of married couples will still be together a year after the baby is born; 75 per cent of cohabiting couples will still be together, but of those who were only 'romantically involved' before the baby arrived, 48 per cent will no longer be together.) Many couples cannot cope with consolidating their own relationships at the same time as taking on this new role of parent.

Food for fuelling relationships

Keep romance alive by going on 'dates' while you still can. Opt for outings where you can interact, rather than going to the cinema or theatre. Restaurants are ideal or just an evening in the pub, if you are short of readies. And, if the budget is very tight, have a date night in: turn off the phone, light some candles, share a meal (nothing elaborate which leaves you exhausted after all the cooking). Share a bowl of strawberries dipped in melted dark chocolate. Very sexy, and satisfies those choccy cravings!

Although not being able to share a bottle of wine is a bummer, you can try a non-alcoholic Bucks Fizz instead (pure, fresh orange juice mixed with sparkling elderflower) and be sure to serve it in champagne glasses!

Relationships under pressure

Why is your relationship under strain when you have a baby? Here are just some of the reasons:

- ❀ Looking after a baby takes a lot of time, which means you have less time for each other . . .
- ❀ . . . you then communicate less with each other and . . .
- ❀ . . . when you don't communicate, misunderstandings arise.
- ❀ Tiredness and lack of communication mean less sex and less intimacy.
- ❀ Couples often find themselves forced into traditional divisions of labour and feel resentful if this division was not made clear beforehand.
- ❀ Postnatal depression (mother or father) can impact on a relationship.
- ❀ A 'difficult' baby exacerbates all of the above.

The pressure of combining work and childcare adds to the modern parents' burden, making life a juggling act in which every moment must be accounted for and there is no time to relax and be together.

Interestingly, mothers become disenchanted with the relationship during the first year after the baby's birth, while for the father, disenchantment sets in during the second year of the baby's life. (Again, the concept that his brain is out of synch with yours by several months!) However, the effect on the father of feeling dissatisfied with his partner is often that he becomes less involved with the baby, and this can generate a negative spiral in that the less involved he is with the baby, the more the mother resents him; he picks up on this and feels even more unhappy with his partner, so he becomes ever-more distanced from the baby and so on.

So it's important to use pregnancy as a time of preparation for the changes in your relationship. Talk about how you were parented. What was important to you about this; what would you like to continue with and what would you reject? Have a look at the

'Hot Topics' on p. 77 and see where you both stand on these. Can you reach a compromise?

And then, looking forward to beyond the babymoon, even though you will be tired and overworked in your baby's first year, it is really important that you make time for each other, and that you keep the channels of communication open. Make a pact to tell each other regularly how you feel. It's not enough to just talk about mundane things, like whose turn it is to load the dishwasher; this is not the sort of communicating you need to do to keep the relationship alive.

Start sharing relationship-building activities during pregnancy, keep one or two going during your babymoon, and ensure that you build more and more of these into your daily life, during your baby's first year:

❀ Go for a walk together every Saturday afternoon with baby in a sling or pushchair and just talk.
❀ Hire a babysitter once a fortnight and get out of the house for a meal together. Babysitting circles are a good idea, where you take turns with other new parents to babysit for each other.

It also helps to:

❀ Take turns to have a lie-in on Sunday morning and recharge your batteries.
❀ Ask your partner for what you need.
❀ Not expect your partner to do everything in the same way you do, but be grateful to each other for the help.

Sex during pregnancy

Some women feel incredibly sexy during pregnancy, while for others it is the last thing on their minds. My suggestion? If you are feeling blooming fabulous (and some women do), go for it like rabbits because you are sure as hell not going to feel much like it for a while afterwards. If it doesn't appeal, well, try and squeeze it in between the morning sickness and the heartburn and focus on ways of being intimate that your poor old body can cope with.

Perhaps you could start things off by practising your massage techniques on each other (see pp. 50–51). That can either lead to more interesting developments or, if you fall asleep in the middle instead, hopefully he will be flattered that he has obviously got the hang of it!

The great thing is that you're pregnant with his baby, so he'll probably be feeling all romantic and attentive. But he'll also be unsure of how sex and pregnancy interact, so will be likely to take his lead from you. Remember that if nothing else, sex will make you still feel fabulously desirable and should help you sleep.

New Family Set-ups

So it is your first baby, but perhaps your partner already has a family? Now is the time to start thinking about these new family ties. Your baby is going to have older brothers and sisters who may be delighted to have a baby to play with, or who might be feeling upset, with their noses out of joint. Even if there is a negative history to overcome, it is really worth trying to foster good relationships with all concerned and being prepared to be adaptable, even if only for your baby's sake. After all, your baby will love all the extra attention bigger siblings can bring. And as far as your partner goes, although there may be an element of 'been there, done that', he will at least have had some experience when it comes to changing nappies, getting babies to settle at night and all that stuff you've got to learn, so bite your tongue when he yawns as you thrust yet another cute picture under his nose.

Your Extended Family

While you and your partner are going through the major transition of becoming parents, your own parents and your partner's parents may also be making a similar transition, if this is their first grandchild.

In many cultures, the grandmother is valued as the key figure preserving and transferring ancestral memories. In the UK, 60 per cent of childcare provision is undertaken by grandparents. The connection your child will have with her grandparents can be an incredibly important one. So it is certainly a good idea to try and get this particular relationship off to a good start.

Although they are now your child's grandparents, they are still your Mum and Dad, and many people find that their bonds with their parents change and deepen when they become parents themselves. Suddenly, you understand why they fussed endlessly about what you were wearing, what you ate and so on. Having said that, if their fussing was a source of irritation before, it may get worse now. While the fussing stems from the best of intentions, for many new parents who are feeling anxious about their role and worrying about doing it right, Granny saying, 'Are you sure she's had enough to eat?' or, worse still, telling them what to do, can be undermining, even if it is well intended.

Finding a way to set boundaries is difficult, but important. One way is to use a fictional friend or health professional: 'That sounds like a great idea, Mum, but the health visitor told me to . . .' or, 'My friend tried this and it worked, so I am giving that a go for the moment; but your idea sounds worth trying if this doesn't work out'. Or you could just try the non-committal, 'I'll certainly bear that in mind'.

Another thing to think about is to what extent your parents may be involved later. Nowadays, many grandparents also act as childminder when Mum goes back to work, which is an incredibly generous thing to do, but it does need explicit accompanying ground rules on both sides. You don't want your mum to feel resentful and put upon, so it is important that she can say just how much she is willing to do and for you to respect that. Also it must be made clear that she can renegotiate that later on, if her feelings change. But you also need to state what you want: if no sweets, no smacking, no guns, no daytime TV are important to you, this does need to be communicated and your mum has to respect it. Try not to be too dogmatic about what you want and don't want though; it does children no harm to experience different rules in different houses – indeed it helps them to develop.

Whatever you decide, you need to talk these issues through before you leave your baby in your parents' care, so everything is clear and out in the open – just as it would be if you were using a childminder or a nanny. Perhaps you and your partner can talk now about how you are going to play it later on.

A PARENT'S TIP

Visitors. We learnt the hard way that you *must* sleep when baby is sleeping, otherwise you'll never catch up on your sleep. We had too many visitors in the first few days and were unable to do this. Spread them out a bit over the second, third or fourth week, they'll understand. You will never have this time together again, just the family getting to know the baby.

Richard, partner of Rosie, and Daddy to Amelie Daisy-May (aged two)

PART TWO

~

Birth: The Beginning of the Babymoon

Your dominant emotion during pregnancy has probably been one of excitement, but perhaps there is also quite a lot of nervous anticipation, even dread at the thought of the birth itself? As the big day gets closer, many women find themselves longing for it to be over, feeling they can't wait for the baby to be born; not perhaps because their fears about the actual birth have changed, but because pregnancy is becoming so uncomfortable, and the build-up has taken so long, that now they just want to get it over and done with.

In this section, we shall see why birth *is* a big deal for women and babies, and why such a long babymoon is needed to recover. In addition, we shall also discover that there is no such thing as a free lunch, in that if you attempt to minimise birth's physical impact, you are in danger of simply swapping one physical ordeal for another. We'll also see that some of the feelings of dread might be the result of birth having been removed to hospitals, so that it is no longer a 'normal' part of life.

Approaching birth as an unknown experience, with the mindset of being helpless and ill – a patient – is not going to help.

One thing this section cannot do is make birth the normal and natural part of your life that it should be, but it can prepare you for what might happen, and it can help you to think about making your birth the best it can be for you and your baby, so that you can begin your babymoon on the optimum footing.

CHAPTER SEVEN

Why birth IS a big deal

So now you have read this far, you may be convinced that a babymoon is a good idea in that it gives you time to get to know your baby. But are you still slightly sceptical about the idea of needing six weeks to recover from the actual birth as well? Are you thinking that with modern medicine and all the wonderful pain-relief options out there, birth should be pain-free and civilised?

Well, the first problem is one of simple physiology. Human babies are big, and our insistence on walking upright has made a small opening even smaller. If we were still crawling around on all fours and giving birth to neat little babies, then yes it might be a doddle, but that's not where we're at.

What evolutionary biologists currently think is that walking upright gave human beings a big advantage over other animals because it freed our hands for using tools; we could throw spears, for instance, allowing us to catch prey which could normally outrun us. And standing upright let us see further ahead; again, pretty useful for hunters. We could gather foods and carry whatever we had gathered using our arms. At the same time, we started to co-operate, so that instead of hunting small creatures down on our own, we could work together, allowing us to catch and eat bigger things. All these important developments meant that we started to evolve bigger brains, which then gave us the extra intelligence to plan, to communicate and, eventually, to create a complicated language as the ultimate tool for working co-operatively.

A bigger brain means a bigger head, *but* walking upright means a narrower pelvis – and, for the women of the species, a problem: how to give birth to a baby with a bigger head through a narrower pelvis?

The solution evolution came up with was for us to give birth to babies at the point when they can *just* fit through (thanks!), but given that we were now being co-operative, we could help each other, rather than just pop the babies out on our own. The other strand to this solution was to shorten the gestation period, so that human babies would be born early (compared to the other ape species). But again, this would be all right, because as a co-operative species we could help each other to take care of these immature babies and nurture the new mother through the baby-moon and beyond.

What evolution did not anticipate, in coming up with this compromise solution, was that we humans would be daft enough to consider that birth could be something you could just do in between finishing off one work project and beginning the next, with a couple of hours break from emails and no babymoon afterwards.

But birth has also become a big deal psychologically speaking. Our ancestors grew up with birth as a natural and normal part of life. Young girls watched older women giving birth; they saw that they were helped by the women around them, that it was possible to give birth with support, that it was something their bodies were designed to do and something to give in to, not to fight through fear. They saw what helps and what doesn't. And this was in the days before we had both access to excellent nutritional advice to help us to grow healthy babies and the safety net of our health-care system.

So despite all our advantages, for modern woman birth is a

journey into the unknown. For many of us, the only images we see of this amazing experience before we actually give birth ourselves are on TV, distorted for dramatic purposes, voyeuristic and far removed from the normal and natural (which, to be frank, would not make terribly interesting TV). To cap it all, it often seems that any friends who have had babies recently tend to tell you the worst bits – the horror stories. This is not because they want to frighten you, but because, for them, the experience is still something that needs to be made sense of, to be processed and, unfortunately, you are there, a captive audience.

Birth is not easy then for human beings, but it works, of course, otherwise we would not be here. Women can and do give birth without medical intervention, and have been doing so for generations. What they have always needed is help from an experienced group of women, and faith in their bodies' ability to give birth.

How Western Medicine Has Improved Birth

It's true that the development of Western medicine has made it possible to save women and babies where birth is not working out in certain cases, through procedures like Caesarean section, for instance. However, the biggest change – the thing that has saved the largest number of mothers' and babies' lives – has come through our understanding of how germs are transmitted and through developing decent hygiene practices. Plus, women often died after childbirth because of postnatal infection which we were helpless to do anything about until the development of penicillin. Better nutrition and higher living standards, along with good prenatal care, have also decreased the morbidity (illness) and mortality rates for women and babies. Today, the women who are at greatest risk from birth in our society are those who come from deprived backgrounds and/or those who do not access prenatal care.

So giving birth in the West today is safer than it has ever

been; not necessarily because of all the interventions available in hospital, but mostly because we generally have a healthier standard of living, anyway. But, as our society has become more risk conscious, hospitals have actually begun to err on the side of caution over, dare I say it, common sense. Caesarean rates in many hospitals are 30 per cent or more, which is far higher than should be expected. Very few births actually proceed without some sort of medical intervention, and many interventions are unnecessary and do not contribute to the health and/or safety of mother or baby. Some are simply a product of hospital protocols, and though most are well meaning, they can be ultimately problematic (for instance, not trusting that the mother can 'cope' and pressing drugs on her until she believes that she needs them).

This latter type of well-meaning intervention can be seen as the result of a sort of vicious spiral: kindly medical person believes woman is not coping; they offer drugs or intervention; woman then takes the drugs or intervention, and kindly medical person now believes that this has helped; so, at the next birth, kindly medical person does the same again and, in the process, reinforces the prejudice in his/her own mind that women cannot cope with birth.

And it is just this 'cascade of intervention' that creates the problem with accepting some sort of medical help during labour. Once you start with intervention, the chances of having another, and then another, becomes more likely. And the ultimate scenario can be Caesarean section or instrumental delivery:

❧ A Caesarean section is major abdominal surgery from which it takes a long time to recover. You will not be able to lift your baby, nor move around without help. You may be given intravenous antibiotics which increase the chances of both you and your baby developing thrush, making breastfeeding excruciatingly painful. And, of course, all major operations carry risks of side effects, including death.

✿ Instrumental delivery means an episiotomy – a cut through the muscles and flesh of your perineum followed by suturing. This, again, is no small thing to recover from postnatally.

Birth statistics

Statistics for 2007–8 show that rates for normal births have fallen over the last two decades. In 2008, around 48 per cent of women who had babies in hospital in England had a normal birth, compared to 60 per cent in 1990; while in Scotland, 39.4 per cent had a normal birth in 2008, compared to 42 per cent in 2001.

Why is Childbirth Painful?

But, I hear you say (and my voice was in there too before I had a baby), surely there is no need to experience pain if there are alternatives?

And yes, there is no point in being a martyr – after all, you would not go to the dentist and willingly have your tooth drilled without anaesthetic. But the pain of childbirth is neither the pain of injury nor the pain that results from surgery; it is a pain that nature has given you resources to cope with. It is also *positive* pain. And I know that sounds very New Age, but it is actually true. If you take away the pain of labour, your body no longer knows what to do, and then you need medical help. However, going with the pain allows your body to mobilise all the hormones it needs, not only to give birth, but also to help you and your baby through the babymoon period.

Take oxytocin, for instance. It's a wonderful hormone; the hormone of love, of orgasm, and also the hormone of birth and breastfeeding. As your baby presses against your cervix and your pelvic floor, you produce oxytocin, which stimulates and sustains your contractions, helping to dilate your cervix and, ultimately, give birth. It then helps you to fall in love with your baby and produce breast milk to feed him. If you take away the sensation of labour, you won't produce that oxytocin.

As pain builds in your body you also produce endorphins, which calm and sustain you through labour, so that when your baby is born you are on a natural high, ready to fall in love with this new person. Suppress the pain and you stop the rise of endorphins.

Many midwives believe that a woman who goes into spontaneous labour at term with a baby in the optimal position for birth (see p. 39) will not experience more pain than she can deal with. And as well as the above, the pain she does experience will also do the following:

- ✿ It is your body's way of alerting you to the fact that you are in labour. You then know to get to a safe place with trusted helpers (see p. 127).
- ✿ Pain directs your body to adopt the best position for your baby. For instance, a particularly sharp contraction might tell you to stand up or to go on to all fours.
- ✿ The sensation of labour and the rising level of hormones also alerts your baby to the fact that he is going to be born. *The hormones are also there to help him cope!* His heart and lungs become primed for life outside the womb, which is one of the reasons why babies born from planned Caesareans (who have not experienced birth hormones) are seven times more likely to have initial breathing difficulties. And the endorphins help him cope with the drop in oxygen that he will experience during second stage.

Suppressing the pain of childbirth

You may be thinking, 'I can't even cope with having my bikini line waxed. Just give me something to take the pain away.' But the problem is that this may well be a case of swapping pain now for pain later.

Epidurals numb you from the waist down, so while it's true that you won't feel anything, having one makes it far more likely (four times more likely, in fact) that you will need an instrumental delivery (and as we saw on p. 93, that means a large cut in your perineum – ouch). You might also be more likely to have an emergency Caesarean at the end (though the evidence is conflicting here). Not a good deal by anyone's standards.

And for those who hate the idea of a needle anywhere near their spine, there are opiates which can give you relief from the pain and allow you to rest, but they can also make you feel sick, out of control and, again, may result in you being unable to push later, which takes you back to the episiotomy/forceps scenarios. Nor are they good for your baby. Pethidine, an analgesic offered as pain relief in labour, is a strong respiratory depressant which concentrates in the baby and can be detected up to seventy-two hours afterwards. Babies whose mothers have opiates during labour are likely to be sleepy for some time after birth and have their suckling reflexes depressed, which means breastfeeding does not get off to the best start.

At this point, you're probably just about ready to hit me, aren't you? But what I'm saying here is that your body *can* do this, and you *can* cope with it (and if you are really struggling to cope with the pain, there are things you can do which will not interfere with your ability to give birth, or affect your baby; see p. 112). So believe this and prepare for labour and birth with this in mind. And the next few chapters will equip you to do just that, so that you can begin your babymoon with only the physical effort of birth to recover from, rather than any major surgery.

A parent's story

It took me nearly two years to get pregnant and my husband and I were beginning to prepare ourselves for IVF. We were on holiday when we found out and could hardly believe it. A sixth sense had told me not to take malaria tablets, despite the negative pregnancy test I had taken before the flight. During our holiday, I remember I was furiously looking up various unusual ingredients we were eating to check that they were OK in pregnancy.

Aside from a slight queasiness early on, my experience of pregnancy was very positive. I felt well, happy and very feminine as my body changed. This sense of wellbeing also enabled me to keep fit by walking every day and I used yoga not only to remain supple, but also to relax. While I did not immerse myself in pregnancy literature, each Saturday morning, my husband and I sat down and found out what the baby was up to in our *Rough Guide to Pregnancy*. The baby could be felt at week eighteen and she was quite a wriggler. Everyone was convinced it was a boy – people from all around the world assured me I would have a son. Only my husband believed otherwise.

An independent midwife supported me through pregnancy, labour and the postnatal period. This gave us confidence to stay at home for the majority of my labour until my midwife suggested hospital. An hour pushing in the labour ward was followed by time on a syntocinon drip. This was not pleasant, and looking back, I wonder whether I should have stayed at home. But we weathered it, with the help of some gas and air. In the small hours of the morning, the nurse was preparing for an episiotomy, when a final contraction urged Niamh into the world. Our daughter was placed immediately on my chest. Those dark little eyes peered upwards! My midwife gently encouraged her to feed. Holding our daughter close and watching this initial feed was indescribably wonderful – the best moment of my life.

Lisa, mother of Niamh (aged two)

~

CHAPTER EIGHT

Thinking about the birth you want

So far we have acknowledged that birth is, indeed, a big deal and that you need your babymoon to recover from it. But we have also – hopefully – established that it is something worth trying to cope with naturally, as the alternatives are not necessarily the easier options in the long term. And perhaps you are now beginning to think there is such a thing as a normal birth, and that you are one of those people who might have one! After all, even though you would be in a minority, it is still a sizeable one (48 per cent in England, just under 40 per cent in Scotland).

In this chapter we will consider in detail what can actually help your birth go swimmingly, so that you come out the other end having avoided the medical interventions. There are several factors which can get you off to the best possible start in labour; the rest will be down to you, your baby, and how you both manage to birth together. It's all about that great Scouting tradition – being prepared (although I'm not sure that Baden-Powell had giving birth in mind when he came up with his slogan). Reading a few chapters in this book and nothing else will, unfortunately, not be enough to prepare you for labour; you'll need to be out there, having a go at things, practising the physical skills you are actually going to need as well as chewing the fat with like-minded people. Where can you do all this? Hopefully, at antenatal classes, so let's start by unpicking what is on offer.

Preparing For a Normal Birth – Antenatal Classes

In order to explore your birth options (in particular finding out what is available in your area), as well as giving yourself enough time to consolidate your thinking about pain management, you're going to have to book and attend antenatal classes, and really, the sooner the better. In addition, you probably don't know many other pregnant women, and antenatal classes create opportunities to network with other new mothers. Practically speaking, there may be potential childminders or nanny shares there too. Friendships made in antenatal classes can last throughout your child's early years and beyond.

Although most antenatal classes are geared to women in the last trimester, there are, as we saw in Chapter Three, exercise classes available throughout pregnancy which can help you prepare your body for labour and birth. Aqua natal, yoga and hypnotherapy classes, for example, start early in pregnancy and continue right up to birth and sometimes beyond.

The duration, cost, content and, indeed, philosophy of antenatal classes vary widely. They will all cover basic information, such as what happens during labour and birth, but that is where the similarities end. What you need to do is to decide what's important to you, and when investigating what's available locally, ask what they cover. Some issues of importance to you might be:

✿ Do they practise positions for optimal foetal positioning (see p. 37), as well as those for a normal or 'active' labour and birth?

- Do they give you an opportunity to discuss the early days as a parent – how to cope with crying, sleeping, and perhaps a chance to talk about routines?
- Breastfeeding – is there a full session on this?

Having found out what's available locally, it might be an idea to go for more than one set of classes, if you can organise the time off work. You will need to book early for most classes.

NHS Parentcraft classes

These are held at your maternity hospital, local clinic, GP's surgery or a community health centre, run by midwives and/or health visitors. They are free, open to everyone and well attended, but as they are often held during the day, dads do not usually go, and indeed in some areas, are not always welcome. What is covered varies widely, depending on the budget for the classes; in some areas of the country they are excellent, in other areas classes have been cut right back. The emphasis will be on procedures in your hospital, as well as the physiology of birth and pain relief. In some areas there will also be sessions looking at feeding and caring for your new baby.

ADVANTAGES OF NHS CLASSES
- They are mostly free, available to all, and local.
- They cover routine procedures in your chosen hospital (so you will at least know what to expect).
- They include a tour of the hospital and the low-down on how to get into the hospital in a hurry!

DISADVANTAGES OF NHS CLASSES
- Classes are usually big and time is limited; this can make it difficult to ask questions or to make friends.
- You may only hear about the hospital's preferred procedures, not necessarily all your options.

❀ Most classes are held during the day, making it hard for partners to attend.

To find out more, speak to your midwife or GP at an antenatal check-up.

NCT classes

NCT (National Childbirth Trust) is a UK-based charity offering private antenatal classes in most areas of the country. (They also have a growing network of teachers in Europe.) These cover similar ground to NHS classes, but with a different approach. Classes are smaller, with an emphasis on group discussions and active learning. Informed choice is a fundamental principle for NCT, so classes cover the pros and cons of various medical interventions, and there are sessions on breastfeeding and parenting issues. While there is certainly encouragement and support for natural birthing techniques, NCT will also prepare you for a managed birth, so that something like an emergency Caesarean will not, hopefully, come as such a shock. NCT is particularly good at developing postnatal support networks. Classes are usually held in the evenings or weekends, and the vast majority of women attend with a birth partner.

Active Birth classes

The Active Birth Centre in London hosts an incredible range of classes, and also co-ordinates a national and international network of Active Birth teachers. Classes are exercise based, to keep you fit and supple during pregnancy in preparation for labour and birth. They aim to give you confidence in your ability to give birth, and will focus on positions for labour, as well as relaxation and massage. Essential information about labour and early parenthood is well covered.

Natal hypnotherapy classes

Natal hypnotherapy courses cover the physiology of birth with a particular emphasis on the emotions of birth. The theory is that in practising hypnosis (being deeply relaxed and listening to positive suggestions and imagery) daily before the birth, you are effectively 'rehearsing' or 'experiencing' in your mind a calm, instinctive birth over and over again. The teachers believe that the mind then does not know the difference between things you have imagined and reality, so that when the actual birth begins, your mind and body are familiar and comfortable with the rehearsed responses and react accordingly. In addition, the hypnosis is conditioning your body to be relaxed and calm, no matter what is going on around you.

Involving your partner in antenatal classes

Many men are initially 'reluctant' to attend antenatal classes, but most agree afterwards that they're glad they went. If your partner is nervous, you could check out with the teacher what is likely to happen, and make sure that other men will also be there. If he is to be any use to you at the birth, he will need to be an informed participant, rather than an embarrassed spectator, as we shall see in Chapter Ten. During labour, you will need to give your body over to the process, which feels a lot easier if someone is there with you who understands you and can look after you.

Note: all working women in the UK have a right to paid time off work to attend antenatal appointments, including antenatal classes which are part of your antenatal care. However, many classes are held in the evenings or at weekends, which also allows partners to attend.

Wonder food – quinoa

This grain might be new to you, but human beings have been eating it for over 6000 years. The Incas thought it sacred, calling it the 'mother of all grains'. It is high in protein, iron and fibre – a real superfood – and, being easy to prepare, it is just what you need to give you energy for birth, and as a nutritious boost during your babymoon. Cook it as you would rice. Try it cold in a salad with feta cheese, spinach and olive oil, or mix it while still warm with a pan full of grilled halloumi cheese, fried leeks (cut into rings), cumin seeds and a squeeze of lemon juice.

A parent's story

I signed up for the natal hypnotherapy course, as I wanted as many tools in my arsenal as possible to help me have a natural birth. Also, like many women, I was worried about how I would cope with the pain. In 2005, I had twins who were delivered by Caesarean section before labour had even started. So although I had two children, I'd never experienced a single contraction and therefore had no idea what the whole experience would be like. And, of course, you hear terrible stories, and all you see in films are scenes of women screaming and everyone panicking!

I bought a set of CDs at the start of the course which I listened to fairly regularly before the birth. They were great for relaxation and full of positive messages. I was so relaxed (or perhaps that was exhausted?) that I often fell asleep while listening. However, my teacher said this was fine and that my mind would still be taking in the positive messages on the CD.

The course was really helpful for preparing my mindset for the birth ahead. It taught me to trust my body; the message was that it knew what it was doing and I should just let it get on with it as much as possible. When the time of the birth arrived, I found I was able to put some of the techniques into practice and that they really helped. In the end, I had a home birth in water, with no pain relief. Although I had a long pre-labour period with two days of contractions, I remained calm and let my body get on with it. I played a CD of music on a loop throughout, which was the same music found in the background of the relaxation CDs, so triggering the positive messages which my brain had taken in previously.

One of my fears had been being unable to push the baby out; worrying that I would not know what to do or how to push effectively. The course made me understand that my uterus was capable of doing all the work; it explained, for example, that women in comas have given birth, obviously without consciously pushing. Of course, it might happen quicker if you do push, but somehow knowing that I didn't have to took the pressure off! During the pushing phase I really relied on the natal hypnotherapy techniques and tried to completely relax my body between contractions.

Although the course is called 'hypnotherapy', it is not about being a zombie or feeling like you are not there. In fact, I would say that I felt incredibly 'present' throughout the entire experience, being a very active participant – much more so than during my first birth when I felt that I was quite passive, having things 'done to me' rather than actively doing anything myself. This birth was the opposite of that.

I would never say that the course meant that I had a pain-free labour and birth. The sensations were intense and I found the whole experience to be very physical, hard work and somewhat brutal. However, I can say that I didn't feel fear or panic during the experience (tired and fed up – yes; but not fearful or panicked). I do believe (as they teach on the course) that a lack of fear and panic can really help a birth to proceed as smoothly as possible.

Elizabeth, mother of Toby and Alexander (aged four) and Jonathan Jago (six months)

CHAPTER NINE

~

What actually happens during birth – and how to cope

Now it's time to see what all the fuss is about. But before we take a closer look at what happens in normal labour, perhaps the first thing we need to know is: what actually is a contraction?

When you experience a contraction, what you are feeling is the sensation caused by muscles at the top of your uterus contracting, pressing down on your baby and also pulling your cervix upwards so it opens. They can be likened to waves in terms of their structure, in that you feel them coming, they build gradually, the sensation getting stronger and stronger, then they reach a peak and die away to nothing. In between contractions there is usually no pain, no sensation; everything is normal and you can talk, move around, change position, cook a roast dinner, learn to tap dance or whatever (well, maybe not the last two!).

So this is unlike any other pain we experience which tends to start suddenly and continue until we do something about it, then fade away with time. The pain of contractions is not sudden or alarming; it comes and goes in a regular pattern with rests in between allowing you to relax and regroup. And while pain from injury is a warning that whatever you are doing needs to stop, labour pain is a creative pain. You may have experienced creative pain if you have pushed yourself physically in other ways: running or exercising hard where you go through the pain to achieve something you did not feel possible, for example.

Labour pain *is* hard to bear, but how it feels depends a lot on what is going on for you. If you were expecting relief with drugs, for instance, which were not allowed for whatever reason, or if it is sudden and frightening and you feel out of control, then it could be unbearable.

Research suggests that women who are not looking forward to having their baby or whose partners are negative about the pregnancy, may feel more pain. If you expect it to be unbearable, then you are likely to be tense and anxious and thus experience more pain. (Remember that experiment with the ice cube, on p. 50?) Whereas – and this concept may or may not do it for you – some people say it really helps knowing that each contraction brings your baby nearer and, best of all, will never need to be repeated. For me, I was not particularly thinking about this, but what I did find useful was that little warning my body was giving me that the contraction was starting, giving me time to focus on relaxing. There was a part of me which actually enjoyed the challenge of coping with it and knowing I was coping with it. I didn't really want to think about how many had come and gone, or how many may still be to come.

As labour progresses, the contractions get stronger, but because it is building steadily, your body gradually gets accustomed to them, and you have time to adjust mentally and to create new coping strategies. Your body will produce endorphins (natural pain relief – see p. 94), which build up as time goes on. It's a bit like running: you start with a walk, then jog, and then you can, eventually, build up to a sprint; but to leap out of your armchair on day one into a sprint would be a hell of a challenge.

There are lots of very effective ways of coping with labour pains which we will be looking at in detail, but first let's look at how labour progresses.

Braxton Hicks

In the days and weeks before you give birth, you might experience 'practice' or 'Braxton Hicks' contractions. These can be strong for some women, while others don't really notice them. They do serve a purpose: they are improving the blood flow to the placenta and baby, as well as contributing to the thinning (effacing) of the cervix. I like to think of them as a limbering-up for your womb; like pre-runs you do before you go on a marathon, every single one helping towards that important end of your baby's birth. They were named after a man (of course) – a Dr John Braxton Hicks, who first noticed them in 1872, apparently. Pardon me for breathing, but I am sure a few women noticed them before that!

What Is Normal Labour?

The start of labour is defined by the powers that be as when you are having regular contractions and your cervix is at least 3cm dilated (which means that those muscles have already pulled your cervix open by nearly a third). Anything that happens before this is defined as 'pre-labour', but it's just as important. In fact, for first-time mothers, pre-labour can be the longest and most difficult part. The only reason it is not 'counted' if you like, is that labour could stop during this stage. In fact, it frequently does if you go into hospital at this point, as adrenaline kicks in and suppresses the other hormones of labour.

The first stage

The first stage of labour ends when your cervix is fully dilated at 10cm. First stage can last any length of time (it can even be quite quick). In advanced stage-one labour, you will no longer be able to chat or do other things, but will be focusing on what is happening to you. The time between contractions will become the time to just relax and regroup ready for the next one.

At somewhere between 8 and 10cm, you go into 'transition', which can be quite weird. What is happening is that your body is getting two contradictory messages. The uterus wants to bear down to give birth, but it's still drawing up the cervix to be fully open. In addition, you are passing out of that dreamlike endorphic state into an alert and ready-for-action state. All of this can cause a lot of confusion, and you may start saying or doing weird things. You might feel physically sick, shaky and cold, and your experience might be that your contractions don't peak and go away, but go on with more than one peak. You might also start to feel angry or upset or that you don't want your baby now. I remember deciding I was going to run away, so I started struggling to my feet (I was kneeling at the side of the bed), and when my partner tried to stop me, I used language I would never, *ever* use in everyday life! It's worth knowing about (and warning your partner about) transition, because quite often people panic and start offering you drugs at this point, whereas if they just waited, everything would calm down again.

The second stage

The second stage is the pushing bit, and lasts about two hours for a first baby, but again this is just a rough guide. It's not continuous for two hours, by the way, in case you are running away in terror – you'll still have contractions at regular intervals with rests in between. But the sensation now is completely different from before. Gone are those waves building, peaking and dying away; now it is about the contractions actually doing something physical, pushing your baby out. At this stage, it is about working with the contractions, so you are in there with them, rather than trying to relax through and almost ignore them if you like, as you do in first stage.

Sometimes, there is quite a long wait at the end of first stage labour before you actually begin second stage. Take advantage of this to recoup your energy, rather than allowing people to hurry you along, and try to get into the optimal position if you can; remember that being upright means your body is working with gravity, rather than against it. Squatting or semi-squatting is helpful, but if you are tired and want to lie down, it is better to lie on your left side, rather than on your back.

It is much better to wait for the urge to push than to force it. The urge to push is a spontaneous reflex; some women don't feel it until right at the end, especially if they are in an upright position, and some feel it before they are fully dilated, usually because the baby is not in the optimal position (see p. 37).

The third stage

The third stage of labour happens after your baby is born, when the placenta and membranes are delivered. But by this stage you have a new baby to think about instead!

Mind Over Matter

As I mentioned earlier, labour is only said to have started once the cervix is at least 3cm dilated. But this can be really disheartening, if you have had hours and hours of contractions up until this point. In fact, for first-time labours, the pre-labour stage is often the longest, and things can move quite quickly once you get established. So don't despair if you have heard that labour will progress at 1cm per hour, and are envisaging another six or seven hours of the same thing! Some women give up and ask for their labour to be managed when they discover they are 'only' 3cm dilated or even less. The temptation at this point is to become disheartened, lie on your back and rest – but this will make it slower and more painful. Those awful stories of people being in labour for days and days come to mind, when what you really need to hear is that it is not long now, your baby will soon be here, just continue to do what you are doing.

So remember: all that pre-labour counts. But it is a bit of a mind game; you are so excited about seeing your baby, and so wound up with what is to come, that you can exhaust yourself too early. Time can pass a lot more quickly if you are feeling calm and relaxed, and if you are still moving around.

It's important to rest between contractions if you feel tired, but also to do things to occupy your mind at the beginning in that pre-labour stage, like going for a walk, watching a video, generally pottering around between contractions.

Feeling tense or stressed during labour is not helpful and can slow down or even stop it. Stress hormones can be helpful in small doses, as they help you adjust to difficult situations and, in this case, help you meet the challenges of labour, but if they are present for too long in your system, you end up feeling exhausted, more anxious and therefore more in pain.

In my first labour, which was in the middle of the night, I played card games with my husband and was completely thrashed – I could only concentrate between contractions, so every three minutes I forgot what I was trying to do in terms of strategy (it was only gin rummy, but you know, I'm competitive). I soon gave up in disgust, as I hate losing! I was so excited about becoming a mum that I was really wound up, and by the time my baby arrived I was exhausted and could barely speak.

My third baby was born on a sunny day after a spell of cold, windy weather. I woke in the morning to regular contractions, so I spent the morning tidying the garden, picking up twigs which had blown off the trees. I leant against the walls of the house as each contraction came, and then resumed the clearing up in between. At this stage, the contractions were mild enough for me to deal with by just relaxing. By this time I had learnt to stay calm, and knew that my baby would put in an appearance soon enough. By the time she was born, I felt tired, but not exhausted, and was able to chat to my other children about their new sister.

Don't dash into hospital too soon 'just to check'. Firstly, your labour may well stop if you do that. Secondly, you end up sitting around there being anxious and excited, and it will wear you out emotionally, so that when you really need your emotional strength it will be gone. Plus, once you are in the system, you are being timed, and therefore there is more likelihood that you will be offered interventions. We'll look at when to go into hospital in Chapter Eleven, but if you feel you cannot relax or feel safe without a midwife near by, go in by all means; once there though, do carry on with keeping mobile and entertained between contractions.

Watching the clock

Everything you read about labour and birth will mention time: 1cm dilation per hour; two hours for second stage for a first baby; one hour for second-time labour; three minutes between contractions; five minutes between contractions, etc. Of course, things will progress in a certain way at a certain pace and rhythm, but becoming too involved in clock watching will take you into your head and your rational self, whereas to give birth you do really need to let go of all that stuff, just for a while.

Your baby will come when she is good and ready, and if you start trying to hurry things, the likelihood of medical interventions will be greater. Even a simple thing like trying to hurry second-stage labour by pushing and holding your breath, is not as helpful as letting nature take its course, because holding your breath to push can reduce the oxygen flow to your baby.

Pain Relief – Coping Strategies

I've said it already, but it is worth saying it again: you *do* have resources for dealing with the pain of labour. And remember, we are not talking about the pain of injury, but a pain that you can understand and come to terms with, one that comes and goes in a predictable pattern, giving you time to adjust and to ready yourself.

Think of the strategies you may already use when you are either in or anticipating pain:

- If you knock a part of your body on something, you rub it better (which does, in fact, serve a purpose, as it encourages blood to flow through that area).
- If you know you are about to have an injection, you take a deep breath, breathe out and relax, look away and think about something else.
- If you have a horrible headache, you take a pill, then lie down in a quiet room to rest and recover.
- If you feel tense and stressed out, or you have aching muscles, you take a long, hot bath.

Most of the above are damned good strategies that can be used or adapted in labour. Let's look at them in more detail.

'Rubbing it better'

This lies at the heart of massage; and hopefully, you have already spent lots of time during pregnancy working out what works and what doesn't for you, as suggested on p. 50.

Breathing / relaxation

We have also had a go at relaxation in Chapter Four, and labour is the time when all this practice is really going to help.

Remember that each contraction will last no longer than ninety seconds (sixty in the early stages) and the breaks between are *much* longer than this. So what you want to do, as you feel a contraction starting, is to take a breath in, and slowly breathe out during the contraction, consciously relaxing your body totally as the contraction builds, peaks and dies away. The quick relaxation technique on p. 49 may help here, and as the contraction starts, drop your shoulders, which will help your body to flop and relax. Focusing on your breath also gives you something to think about rather than focusing on the intensity of the contraction.

Take a pill and lie down in a dark room

We will look at pain relief for labour later on (see p. 116), but as this is a constructive pain, taking a pill is not really your best first option. And as for lying down in a dark room and waiting for it to go away? Appealing, but probably not the most useful strategy here. The dark room might be helpful, and we will look at the importance of the environment in the next chapter. But lying down? Not a good idea. As we've already seen (see p. 109), gravity can help your baby descend: if you are lying down, you are working against gravity, while by being upright you get gravity on your side. Better still, leaning forward helps your uterus to be more efficient, as each contraction pushes the womb *forward* in order to push your baby *down*. If you lie down, your backbone gets in the way of this. Then, in second stage, lying flat on your back makes the pelvis narrow, whereas being upright or leaning forward, or going on to all fours, helps the pelvis open, making it easier for the baby to come out. Lying on your back for pushing also makes it more likely that you will tear.

In the first stage of labour the contractions are about opening up your cervix, while for your baby, it is about her turning to the optimum position for being born (if she is not already there – see p. 37). So you can help both of these to happen by staying upright and letting gravity move your baby into the pelvis. The sensation of pressure also helps your body to produce the hormones you need to make the contractions work. You don't need to be standing still though – you can try rocking and swaying through the contractions.

Leaning forward with your legs apart widens the pelvis giving your baby the optimum space to manoeuvre in. It is a particularly helpful position if you have back pain. You might want to lean forward over your birth ball, the edge of the bed or, perhaps, over your partner while he sits in a chair facing you. Oddly enough, sitting on the toilet the wrong way round can be helpful, leaning on the cistern (although you'd probably want a thick towel or blanket across the seat for comfort).

Try different things. See what works at any one moment in

time and keep experimenting and changing (or get your partner to remind you to do this) to find what feels most comfortable. Sometimes labour goes slowly or even stops, and changing your position can get it started again or speed things up.

A hot bath

An excellent idea. Many women find getting in the bath really helps to ease the pains of labour. In most hospitals, you'll have access to a bath, although again, you should check this on the ward visit. You can, of course, just jump into your own bath at home for pain relief. I got in the bath to ease the pains in first stage and noticed that the water, even when the bath was full, did not cover my enormous bump! And I really needed that bit of me to be under water to feel any benefit. So I ended up sticking a flannel into the overflow and wedging it there with my toe. I also soaked a small towel in the hot water and draped it over my tum to keep it wet and warm. You could use plasticine to block the overflow, which might be more efficient than a flannel-and-toe arrangement.

Birth in water

A lot of women find water so comforting that they end up staying in for the actual birth. There is growing evidence to support this as a practice, but only if you are using a proper birthing pool where the water comes up to your breasts when sitting upright. When birthing under water, women spontaneously lift and thrust forward, and if the water is too shallow, there is a danger that the opening to the vagina might come into contact with cold air. Then the baby would gasp, which is bad news if she is under water.

Many hospitals have special birthing pools, but, unfortunately, they operate on a first-come, first-served basis so there is no guarantee you'll get access to it. This is something to check out on that ward visit, if you are particularly keen on the idea of a water birth. You can also hire a special birthing pool to use at home, either before you go into hospital or to use at a home birth; Google 'water birth' for your nearest supplier. You will need a good hot-water supply, and you might need to check out your floorboards to ensure that they can support the weight of a pool full of water.

When You Need Extra Help (But Don't Want Drugs)

If you are really struggling to cope with the pain of contractions, there are various things you can do which will not interfere with your ability to birth, and will not affect your baby. It is worth thinking through these options now, at this stage, and mentioning any extra help you would consider on your birth plan (see p. 132).

TENS machine

There is plenty of evidence that the TENS (transcutaneous electrical nerve stimulation) machine works but there is no hard evidence as to *why*. Some say it stimulates your body's natural painkillers (endorphins), others say it works as a distraction because it gives you something else to think about during contractions. You need to start using it at the beginning of labour for it to be effective, and you will not be able to get into the bath if you are using it. However, it has no side effects, and you can always take it off later on if you are finding it too much of a distraction. If you are the sort of person who loves gadgets, give it a go!

Gas and air

Gas and air (or Entonox) is inhaled and self-administered during each contraction and clears afterwards, so there is no residual effect. It takes the edge off the peak of the contraction; you feel woozy and light-headed, but your brain clears as soon as you stop inhaling the gas and you go straight back to normal. So there's no danger that you'll take too much because once it takes effect, you just won't want to breathe it in any more. (Off the record, it's a bit like being momentarily, pleasantly stoned, only without the munchies!) All labour wards have gas and air piped in through the walls, and if you have a home birth your midwife will bring it for you in cylinders.

A revitalising smoothie for when you are tired and in need of nurturing

Make a mug of hot chocolate, then whizz it together with one ripe banana, a teaspoon of honey, a pinch of nutmeg and a pinch of cinnamon. Stir with a cinnamon stick and sip through a straw when your labour seems endless.

Acupuncture

Acupuncture in labour is becoming increasingly popular as a form of pain relief which does not interefere with natural birth. Acupuncturists recommend commencing treatment before labour to allow the beneficial effects to build up in the body in advance. During the actual labour, needles are inserted in points in the ear, rather than in the body, to avoid restricting movement. If you think you might like to try acupuncture, contact a registered practitioner any time from thirty-six weeks onwards (see Resources, p. 230).

A parent's story

Lulu was born at twenty-seven weeks and five days' gestation by Caesarean section, late on in a largely silent labour. She was tiny by the standards of a full-term baby (only 1.1kg), but well by the standards of extremely premature babies. She nevertheless needed respiratory support for five weeks after birth, spent most of each day in an incubator until seven weeks and was primarily fed my milk through a naso-gastric tube.

Her birth and early days passed in the most medicalised environment possible, attended by fourteen obstetric and neonatal staff in the high-dependency room of a large neonatal unit. Parents of term babies are shocked that our daughter was twenty-four hours old before I held her; parents of premature babies are amazed that I was permitted to do so.

I was told early in the day that I could hold her, and to wear something that unbuttoned down the front. I had to wait until my husband visited, because I could not make the journey to the neonatal unit by myself so soon after delivery. Lulu's nurse, a quiet, gentle woman, removed some of the wires and probes attached to her body and took her out of the humidity tent she was in. Then I truly saw her for the first time: red, as all extremely premature babies are, and covered in downy hair, her etiolated limbs flung wide and her dark eyes staring. I smelled her, and knew she was mine. Once I felt her on my skin, tiny and hot, I never wanted to let her go.

I know now that we were fortunate that our daughter was born in a hospital that actively supports kangaroo mother care, and that this early contact fostered many things – my body's ability to make milk to feed her, her ability to breathe and regulate her temperature, and our confidence in caring for our daughter. We understood very early on that this was not 'just a cuddle', and once she came home, eight weeks old and four weeks before her due date, continued to spend large parts of each day breastfeeding, cuddling or carrying her close to us. This was partly a conscious choice – she had been deprived of physical contact, so leaving her alone in a cot did not seem right – and partly necessity, since she was still physically tiny at 2kg and I could not have coped with feeding her day and night without the extra minutes of sleep gleaned by bed-sharing.

Just over three years later, our second daughter was born at thirty-eight weeks' gestation. I had feared the postnatal period, knowing how relentless the cycle could be. But the days after her birth, during a babymoon enforced by another emergency Caesarean, were truly euphoric. She spent most of our time in hospital in bed with me – the difficulties of manipulating a hospital gown and the heat meant I spent most of my time effectively naked. I was in a side room, and as I had no particular difficulties with anything, we were largely left alone together. One thing intrigued me: whenever I tried to place her between my breasts, in the position I had been taught for kangaroo care, she would wriggle across my chest, looking for the nipple, in a feeding reflex I had heard described, but had never seen.

I felt a powerful and complex mix of emotions: I had really, really wanted to avoid another section, I was, in truth, relieved that my pregnancy was over, but most of all, I was falling head over heels in love with my baby daughter in the most primal and sensual way. She was an April baby, so in my memory I think our first days together will always be bathed in spring sunshine.

Liza, mother of Lulu (aged three and a half) and Carla (four months)

Influencing your birth experience

S O FAR WE HAVE LOOKED at how birth works and how to cope with it, as well as thinking about how to prepare through choosing the right antenatal classes. In this chapter, we are going to concentrate on thinking about the environment that is right for you; where to give birth and who to have with you to help.

Birth Environment

Arguably, where you labour and give birth is the most important factor in the equation. If you don't feel safe in a place, you cannot relax; and, as we have seen earlier (see pp. 109–10), being able to relax is vital in allowing labour to progress and also in coping with pain and tension.

It's the same with other aspects of your life – your home, your work, where you go on holiday – the environment is such a big factor in whether or not you are happy, isn't it? So why not think about it now: the place where this momentous thing is going to happen, and where you are going to welcome this new member of your family?

Where to Give Birth

Until the advent of the National Health Service, everyone gave birth at home. And while home might not have been the cleanest place, at least it was somewhere you felt safe and comfortable, and where everything you wanted or needed was to hand, and the dirt and germs were your own. Nowadays, most women give birth in hospitals, and it's easy to forget what a radical change that has brought about. It has meant that birth has moved out of the normal world, and into the medical/sickness/patient world. While many women feel safer being in a hospital, knowing that life-saving expertise and equipment are at hand, it does mean that they start the whole experience with the mindset of being ill, helpless and with other people in charge. It also means entering the system of clock watching and routines – again, not the most relaxing frame of mind for birth to progress naturally.

Making a hospital birth work for you

What does the word 'hospital' mean to you? Are the associations mostly unpleasant – things like illness, pain and death? These are not necessarily concepts you'll want at the back of your mind when you are in labour!

It is a good idea to visit the maternity unit early on in your pregnancy (regular ward visits are arranged for expectant parents, so just find out when the next one is and tag along). See how you feel about that environment. What does it smell like to you? Sounds like a mad question, but in labour you are going to get back to fairly basic levels, and smell is a very primitive sense. Could you feel in control or will you feel vulnerable? What could you do to make the place work for you – to make it your own space (more on this on pp. 125–6)?

Consider the layout of the room in which you would labour and give birth: is there a large bed smack in the middle of a small space, giving you no option but to hop on it and spend the entire time on your back? Is all the equipment obvious and centre stage or is it tucked discreetly out of the way? Can the lighting be dimmed? Can you feel private and safe in this space?

You may well be pleasantly surprised. Hospitals have changed dramatically in the last few decades, and birth is treated in many places as a normal event, where women are mobile during labour, welcome to birth in water, with only midwives in attendance.

Small birthing units

Even if the hospital looks fabulous, it is still worth exploring the alternatives. In many areas, there are small units called birth centres or GP units (which are actually run by midwives). They are perfectly safe places, where you are not made to feel sick or in danger, but these are not as well publicised as they might be, particularly for first-time births. Have a look at this option before plumping for the main hospital (Google 'birth centres' and a plethora of resources will appear).

Home births

You could also think about a home birth. Only 2.5 per cent of women currently give birth at home in the UK, although statistics vary across the country. The point is that you do have a legal right in the UK to a home birth, so if you feel it is something you want to consider, your midwife should discuss it with you. You might also want to get support from your local home-birth support group (see Resources, p. 231).

If you are hoping to have a home birth, your midwife needs to be someone you like and trust. This could be your community midwife or it might be a private one. For full autonomy and to guarantee the presence of a known midwife you'd probably need private care, which is not a cheap option, but one you might want to consider. (In fact, it's a legal requirement to have two midwives at a home birth, the second one being called in once the birth is imminent. In terms of cost, however, you just pay for one.)

A home birth does not make you a lentil-weaving hippy or a dangerous, selfish nutter who is putting herself and her baby at risk. There is plenty of solid evidence to show that a planned home birth is just as safe for mother and baby as a hospital birth, and that it will have fewer interventions. Remember that hospital births have evolved in the UK by default, not through any medical evidence to prove that it is the best option. One third of all women in the Netherlands have home births and their statistics are as good if not better than ours.

How safe are home births?

It is true that in a hospital there is life-saving equipment on hand for the tiny number of babies who need it. But midwives who attend home births are also equipped to deal with most emergencies, including baby not breathing and mother haemorrhaging. Babies still do die in hospitals unfortunately, and the problem is that births can become complicated and risky simply as a result of being in hospital than would otherwise happen. Partly, this has to do with how a woman feels about her environment: feeling tense or stressed during labour can slow it down or even stop it.

There are also those time-based hospital protocols, whereby a certain amount of time is 'allowed' for second stage (before your baby is delivered by forceps or ventouse), your cervix is expected to dilate within a certain amount of time (after which your labour may be artificially sped up) and your waters are sometimes broken artificially after a certain amount of dilation . . .

There is also the real risk of hospital infections, where you are exposed to more and different germs from those you are already used to in your own home.

Advantages of a home birth

- ❀ You are on your own territory, so you are more likely to relax and feel in control.
- ❀ You are not going to be offered any unnecessary interventions, as you are with hospital protocols.
- ❀ Those who are with you are guests, not in control.
- ❀ Midwives are in charge, not obstetricians.
- ❀ Your partner and your family are a part of the experience, not passive bystanders.
- ❀ Afterwards, the family can be together, as opposed to you and your baby being in the hospital ward, while the rest of the family is 'sent home'.

Choosing a home birth: an informed choice

If you are going to opt for a home birth or indeed, birth in a small birthing centre, you have to be well prepared to cope with labour. You need to be willing to be in control of your own labour, not handing it over to someone else, so attending independent antenatal classes is a really important first step, as well as reading up everything you can ahead of time.

Some nourishment for when labour is long

A sustaining smoothie

Blend together 235ml milk, 40g oats, 1 banana, 14 frozen strawberries.

High-energy snacks

- ❀ Bananas
- ❀ Jelly cubes
- ❀ Dates (and other dried fruits)
- ❀ Coconut
- ❀ Sweetened oatcakes

Making Your Chosen Environment Your Own

Wherever you decide to give birth, it is a good idea to have lots of props ready. For instance, you may want to listen to music, so it is worth loading an iPod with different-style playlists – relaxation, energising, whatever you think might work for you. You might also want to have a CD player and CDs, in case you don't like being cut off by headphones. Remember, in hospitals they don't like you plugging in untested electrical items, so you'll need lots of spare batteries.

Musical labour

I would imagine that any effect that music might have must depend on what you choose. When we went into hospital to have our first baby, they kindly provided a CD player for our use, and we discovered the previous couple had left their choice of music behind – Leonard Cohen! Hard to imagine that this could be tremendously helpful with labour pains, but each to their own, I guess . . .

Suggested 'props' for hospital births

- ✿ Birth ball
- ✿ Cushions
- ✿ Massage oils
- ✿ TENS machine, if you're planning to use one (see p. 117)
- ✿ CD player/iPod
- ✿ Lip balm and face cream; hospitals are hot and will dry you out
- ✿ Spare batteries for everything
- ✿ A hand mirror (you might want to see your baby emerge)
- ✿ Camera
- ✿ A water mist spray

- ❀ A battery-operated fan
- ❀ Swimwear for partner (in case you decide to use the birthing pool and he wants to get in with you; hospital rules require he covers up his naughty bits)
- ❀ Crop top or vest for you if you are going in a birthing pool and don't want to be 100 per cent naked
- ❀ Long, baggy T-shirt to give birth in and socks for cold feet (I know I said the hospital is hot, but for some reason my feet were freezing)
- ❀ Something for your man to eat – they might feed you, but they certainly won't feed him; he'll get hungry and tetchy and wander off to look for something to eat just at the wrong moment; he'll need something to do as well as there is a lot of hanging about
- ❀ A bottle of water and some bendy straws for you to sip it (or other drinks) during labour
- ❀ High-energy drinks and snacks (see p. 124)
- ❀ Change for the phone – some hospitals won't let you use your mobile
- ❀ Champagne (and glasses – unless you want to quaff from the bottle)

Even if you are planning to birth at home, you'll still need to get all your gear together so that everything is to hand, and perhaps have a holdall ready to throw things into, in case you transfer. It is a good idea to look around your house and think about props for kneeling or squatting. Doorways? Banisters? I knelt at the side of our bed with a spongy, doubled-over exercise mat under my knees – it can get sore kneeling for a long time! (I also used the mat to spare the carpet, but in fact the midwife arrives with tons of stuff for mopping everything up and not a spot is left anywhere.)

Think about the lighting at home too. You might want it dim and cosy, but it's an idea to have a small lamp on a table near by for the midwife to use. And temperature is another consideration;

you may feel hot or cold, so both a fan to cool you down and a fan heater to heat everything up quickly (especially when the baby is imminent) are both useful.

If you are going into hospital, practise your positions at home first, and ask your birth partner to help you adopt these when you get there. Don't forget your birth ball to sit on or lean over, and perhaps take a mat for kneeling on, or cushions.

Who is Likely to Be With You When You Give Birth?

While history tells us that birth was often a risky business for our ancestors, one thing we do know is that there were lots of women there to help – a midwife, friends and family members. And this is still the case in the developing world. In our culture, these women were called God sibs (or sisters in God), which was later corrupted to 'gossip' – interesting that such a negative term grew out of something so helpful! The main difference between then and now was, of course, that the labouring woman knew all these women, gossips or God sibs. This is unlikely to be the case for you, unless you engineer it.

Hospital midwives

It is worth pointing out that with a hospital birth, your midwife might actually be a man. Statistically speaking it is unlikely, but there are a growing number of male midwives now. If this is something that makes you feel uncomfortable, it is a good idea to ask now if there are any male midwives on the unit and to discuss your fears and options in this respect.

If you are going to give birth in a main maternity hospital, once you have been admitted in labour, you will be assigned one midwife, who may also be caring for several other women in labour at the same time. In the early stages, she may well come and go, depending on how you are doing. She may also be replaced once or even twice by new midwives as shifts change. If you are having a water birth, a second midwife will join you once you reach second stage; one to look after you, one for the baby. (There are always two midwives for home births as well.) If complications develop (if you need forceps or ventouse, for example) the duty doctor, consultant or a paediatrician may be called in. For more potentially complicated labours like twins, prematurity or a breech baby (when the baby is born feet first, rather than head first – see p. 37), there will be several people involved throughout your labour.

Knowing your midwife

One of the advantages of home birth or birth in a small unit, is that you will already know the person or people who will be with you in labour. They will be responsible for your antenatal care and thus you will have formed a relationship with them, having met them during pregnancy. This is unlikely to be the case in hospital, despite years of research supporting the claim that knowing the person with you in labour is tremendously helpful. Women who labour with a known midwife need less pain relief, fewer interventions, have shorter labours, are more satisfied with their care and feel more confident and more prepared for the birth and care of their baby. There are also significant reductions in the use of epidurals. Numerous government initiatives have tried to create systems whereby you would know your midwife in advance, but nothing to date that has worked. Some women have been known to book home births simply to ensure that continuity of care from their community midwife, because if you end up transferring to hospital from a home delivery, your midwife goes with you.

Some areas of the country operate a domino scheme (short for **dom**iciliary midwife **in** and **o**ut) whereby you are looked after antenatally and in early labour by your own community midwife, who then accompanies you in to hospital for the actual delivery, and takes you home again afterwards. In Powys, Wales, community midwives attend early labour and only make the decision there and then as to whether a domino or home birth is appropriate. This innovative idea has brought their home-birth rate up to nearly 12 per cent, and means that all their clients are able to experience continuity of care. Talk to your community midwife about all your options.

Other birth attendants

You may have an experienced woman friend or relative who is prepared to be with you through birth, and this is a great option to consider, but if this is not possible, you might want to consider employing a doula. This is a woman who has given birth, who is not medically qualified, but who has been trained to accompany and support women in labour. They do not assist with the actual birth; their role is simply to support you in labour. They also help you after the birth at home – think of them as the experienced granny or sister who would have been with you in a traditional setting.

You may be thinking that things are beginning to sound a little crowded, but it is becoming more acceptable to have a second birth partner with you in hospital apart from your own partner. Check it out first with your hospital though. If you do have a second birth partner coming with you, it might be useful if she attends antenatal classes with you.

Your partner's role (or not) in birth

There is now a widely held assumption that the baby's father will be at the birth, but this is, actually, a relatively recent trend. Fathers throughout history were traditionally shoved off somewhere to do something else: down to the pub or off to the kitchen to boil water, when home births were prevalent in the UK, while in some cultures they had rituals to undergo to mark their transition to parenthood, all of which took place well away from the actual birth. The birth itself was seen as something entirely female.

You may think that having your baby's father at the birth is a matter of choice, but the role he plays once he is in there is pretty much still culturally determined. My father wanted to be present for my birth, but this was virtually unheard of at the big London hospital where I was born in the 1960s. In the end, he was stuffed into a white coat and mask and tolerated, as long he kept out of the way – until staff decided things were getting tough and he was bundled outside.

The fact that men are now more welcome at birth is viewed cynically by some – is he simply an extra person to help in an understaffed hospital? (My partner certainly had hospital expectations thrust upon him, when he was treated as an essential extra pair of hands and eyes, watching monitors while staff busied themselves in other areas of the hospital.) But I think it is also about men's changing role in society. Looking back at the time when men were not encouraged to attend births, their role was very traditional – that of breadwinner, pillar of strength, but definitely not someone who was allowed to show emotions. Nowadays, it's OK – desirable even – for men to be more emotionally intelligent, able to access and express their emotions, while still being capable of being strong and supportive, as well as being the financial breadwinner, if that is what the relationship needs. In addition, men today play a far larger part in raising children than their fathers did, so why not begin with the birth? Part of having your partner fully involved might mean that he would prefer to be the person who cuts the cord and identifies the sex of your baby, so this could be something you also put on your birth plan (see p. 132).

Some people now argue that for the man, being at the birth is difficult, as they must stand helplessly by and watch the woman they love in pain, and that perhaps they even run the risk of being traumatised by what they see and hear. I have not heard of any man who has *not* been emotionally affected by being there at the birth of their own child; yes it may be traumatic if the birth is traumatic – but then who is to say how they would be affected by being left in the corridor and not knowing what was going on?

Men can feel uncomfortable in hospital. The staff may try to co-opt them to get their partners to 'comply' or they may feel they are the lone voice fighting for whatever was wanted in the labour and birth. Either way, this creates enormous pressure, and can leave the man feeling torn or guilty.

Then there is the whole man and machine thing: some men will feel very reassured by all the technology and equipment in the birthing room, while many women will feel uncomfortable with it, so that the two of you may start off on different footings. If he is that way inclined, perhaps he will put pressure on you to have the interventions that are offered.

On a positive note, in a hospital birth your partner's may be the only familiar face with you, and that can be tremendously comforting.

If you want your partner to be there, it is therefore best if he is preparing for the birth throughout your pregnancy, as you are. This is why you should prioritise any antenatal classes that actively encourage his attendance and participation, so that you can both be equally well informed about birth and have formed shared ideas about how your child should come into the world. Your partner should be fully informed about how labour works, about positive pain (see pp. 105 and 93) and, of course, he should have practised optimal foetal and labouring positions with you (see p. 37), as well as being up on all his massage techniques (see p. 50).

Yes he should be there if . . .

✓ . . . he's been to antenatal classes, and he knows his stuff.

✓ . . . he knows what you want, understands your birth preferences and will argue for your choices, if necessary.

✓ . . . you are happy for him to see you at your worst.

✓ . . . there is no one else you would rather have.

Don't let him near you if . . .

✗ . . . he doesn't want to be there.

✗ . . . you will feel inhibited.

✗ . . . he's really squeamish, and gets freaked out by hospitals and doctors.

✗ . . . he has strong views which conflict with your own.

Ultimately, it is your decision. You might choose to have more than one person if you want, so by all means leave him behind and bring mother, mother-in-law and the neighbours too if you want – but be prepared for some raised eyebrows!

Involving other children

If you already have a child or children, you will be thinking about how to involve them in the arrival of their new sibling; you will have been talking to them during pregnancy, perhaps allowing them to feel the kicking and so on. So what role will your children have during the birth?

If you are having a home birth and want them to attend, it would be a good idea to prepare them: talk about what will happen and how you might be. You will need to have another adult on hand (besides your partner) to be with your child during the birth. It is unlikely that your child will want to stay with you the whole time, anyway, so someone will have to be there to play with them if they get bored and want to go off and do other things. If you are at home, you will still need someone to babysit, in case you are transferred to hospital.

Birth Preferences

Having decided how you would ideally like your birth to go, it is important that those around you are also aware of it. Talk it through with your birth partners beforehand, visit the hospital together and imagine yourselves in there: how might you cope? What strategies are in place?

If you already have a relationship with the person who will be helping you give birth, it may not be essential to write everything down, as you will have discussed it all with them already. If you are going to be in hospital, however, probably with unknown midwives, you might want to write a formal birth plan to save you having to explain yourself to several different people. Most midwives are happy to go with a birth plan and like to see one, so don't feel you are being awkward.

When preparing your birth plan, it does help if you express yourself positively, rather than confrontationally: 'I would like X, Y and Z', rather than, 'I demand' or, 'You must/must not'. Things you might think about writing down are interventions you would prefer to avoid and any alternatives you would suggest and any positions you want to try. If you have a doula, she can help you write your birth plan and also be your advocate for it when you are in labour.

If you have any particular feelings about the third stage, these need to be recorded, otherwise it will be assumed that you are happy to have a managed third stage. (This is where you are injected with syntometrine to close down the uterus, and the cord is clamped and cut quickly, as opposed to the physiologic third stage, where things happen naturally; the pros and cons of each should be explored in antenatal classes.) It is also worth asking for your baby to be delivered on to your stomach, although most hospitals would assume you want this, unless you state otherwise.

You might also want to include some thoughts about a Caesarean in your birth plan: if it happens, how would you like it to be (see box overleaf)? Incidentally, in some London hospitals, 'natural' Caesareans are being undertaken, whereby the baby is lifted out slowly, giving him time to adjust, parents can see everything and the baby is immediately placed skin to skin. It is a good idea to find out whether these new practices are used in your hospital.

Caesarean birth plan

Here are a few suggestions as to what you might specify should you have a Caesarean:

- ✿ I would like my partner to stay with me throughout.
- ✿ I want to hold my baby as soon as possible after birth, and if I should require a general anaesthetic, I would like my partner to remain near by and for the baby to go straight to him.
- ✿ I would like the curtain to be dropped, so we can see what is going on.
- ✿ I would like the theatre to be as quiet as possible during my baby's birth.
- ✿ I would like to play a certain CD when my baby is born (you should be able to welcome your baby into the world in an environment of your choosing, even if this is also an operating theatre).

What Can Your Partner Do to Help With Pain Relief? (Get Him to Read This Bit!)

If your partner is going to be your birth companion, it's really important that he understands why labour pain is purposeful, and why it is not a good idea to remove it, so get him to read Chapters Seven and Nine, in particular. It's not fair to expect him to witness you in pain, if he does not realise what is going on.

Hopefully, you will be spending lots of time during pregnancy practising massage and relaxation with your partner (see Chapter Four). But both of you should be aware that up to 70 per cent of women in active labour don't want to be touched, so that it does not come as a shock if you threaten him with decapitation when he approaches you with the massage oil.

Here is a list of suggestions to stick under your birth partner's nose now:

- As she breathes out at the beginning of the contraction, she needs to drop her shoulders, which will help her body to flop and relax. You can remind her to do this by pressing on her shoulders as the contraction starts.
- Look out for signs of tension – is her jaw clenched? Are her fists clenched? Lay your hands on her body where it is tense, to remind her to relax.
- It will be helpful if you talk to her during labour, reassuring her that she's doing well. Not too verbose; she won't want to feel bullied. Just let her know you are there for her, using words of gentle encouragement.
- On that point, if you are not sure, ask her what she wants between contractions, but offer these as either/or choices to avoid breaking her concentration. So rather than saying, 'What do you want now?' ask, 'Would you like a sip of water?' or, 'Would you like a massage?' or, 'Is this touch strong enough for you?'
- Massage: you've practised this during pregnancy, so you know what she likes and dislikes, right?
- Positions for labour: again, you will have practised these in antenatal classes, but here are a few reminders:
  - Sit behind her and support her in an upright position. You might, in this position, stroke the front and sides of her lower abdomen.
  - Sit on a chair facing her while she kneels in front of you and leans forward, so you can support her. Or she can sit with her back to you on the birth ball and you can then massage her lower back.
  - If available, sit on the stairs with your legs open and her sitting on the stair below you and between your legs, so you can support her with her underarms resting on your knees.
  - Keep reminding her to change position, as well.

- Encourage her to eat and drink little and often.
- Remind her to go to the toilet frequently.
- And remember – she might swear or shout at you, blame you for how she feels and generally let off steam in your direction. Try not to take it personally!

Packing a Bag for Longer Hospital Stays

Most women nowadays are ushered home quite quickly after the birth, as the hospital needs the space. However, if you or your baby has complications you may need to stay in for longer, so it's useful to have a bag ready packed for your partner to bring in to tide you over that stay. These are things you might want to pack:

- A long nightie – you will probably lie on top of the bed, as it will be too hot to stay under the covers and you don't want to scare the visitors!
- A long dressing gown for when you want to pad around the place. You will probably feel quite vulnerable walking around in just a skimpy nightie. Also you'll need slippers or non-slip socks; you don't want to end up flat on your back on the polished floors.
- Lots of industrial-strength sanitary towels. You can't use tampons. I suggest also buying some granny-type knickers – you'll want a really high waist (in case you've had a Caesarean; see also Resources, p. 231) and you may well leak on them, so get cheap ones you won't mind throwing out afterwards.
- Ear plugs and sleep mask. (Don't worry, you will hear your own baby; you just don't want to hear everyone else's.)
- A soft bra top for the first few days like a sports bra or sleeping bra, and then nursing bras and breast pads for when your milk comes in.
- Reading material. Your baby might sleep, but you probably won't. However, there is no point in tackling anything heavy duty – you won't be able to concentrate – so just take

magazines for skimming through, or ideally, all those leaflets you have been accumulating through pregnancy, but haven't actually read yet! You won't have time to do this again for a good few months. Take some motivational books as well. I read a breastfeeding book in the wee small hours when everyone was asleep and I was awake and breastfeeding; it motivated me to keep going when I thought I would chuck it all in.

- A nice outfit to wear when you are going home. You want to feel special.
- Mobile phones are not always allowed in hospitals, but there are pay phones, so take plenty of coins. There is often a phone by your bed to use as part of a package with radio, TV, etc., but this can be expensive (and I'd suggest you ask how much it costs for people to ring *you* too).
- Food. Hospital food is invariably disgusting and often comes at the wrong time anyway, with nothing available in between. Get your partner to bring you fresh fruit (remind him to wash it beforehand) and other goodies.
- And on that point, you might want to bring your own teabags (unless you actually like tea that can strip tooth enamel).
- Antiseptic wipes to clean toilet seats and moist toilet tissue – loads of it.
- A wash bag with toothbrush, toothpaste, tissues, hairbrush, hair ties, etc.
- Baby clothes. Stick to vests, nighties or very thin layers, as the hospital will be hot.

A parent's story

After three previous straightforward births, two of them at home, I was looking forward to my fourth baby's arrival and feeling positive and confident.

I was due Christmas Day, but by 2 January, there was still no sign, so my midwife came round and performed a membrane sweep for me [see p. 146]. After she left, I felt very crampy and began to suspect things were happening. During the evening I started having contractions about every ten minutes and they were noticeably higher up than the usual practice ones. If I paced up and down, it seemed to intensify the contractions, but it was getting late and my husband (Stuart) suggested that instead of keeping the labour going by moving around, we try and get a night's sleep and do it in the morning! This seemed like a sensible idea, so we went to bed. I soon fell asleep and during the night I only woke two or three times with contractions. I woke about 6 a.m. and knew that as soon as I got up things would start up again. I lay there peacefully enjoying the quiet and feeling my baby wriggle in my tummy.

We realised when we got up that Stuart should stay home from work. My son went off to my sister's, and my good friend Rachel collected the girls, so they'd all gone by about 8.30 a.m., all very happy and excited.

Then there was a bit of a lull and I started to wonder whether it was going to be a long time before things picked up. Stuart and I sat and watched a bit of *Love Actually*, but I soon went upstairs and had time on my own listening to relaxing birth music and alternating between walking up and down, bouncing on the birth ball and leaning up against the chest of drawers. The contractions were about every five minutes, but not long.

When the first midwife came, she examined me and I was pleased when she told me I was 8cm dilated. I then carried on doing my thing while she pottered about. About an hour later, the second midwife arrived. I felt sick and very weepy. I was still breathing through the contractions and saying '3–2–1 relax' to myself. Stuart was rubbing my back, which was lovely. The midwives went downstairs and left us alone and it was the nicest time; I seemed to be coping so well that the midwife thought the contractions had stopped! I really did feel in control and so positive. I actually enjoyed parts of it and I felt confident that it was all progressing as it should. But as time wore on and the baby hadn't arrived, I began to get a bit fed up.

I instinctively believed that as soon as my waters broke the baby would be born and was trying to stand and move to encourage them to go. I told the midwives this and they suggested that maybe in half an hour's time they could break my waters. I replied that half an hour seemed like a long time, so one of them examined me. I was fully dilated and the baby was well down, so she quickly popped the waters.

Immediately, things sped up and the baby began moving down. I was sitting up on the bed but I had no desire to push at all. I was squeezing Stuart's head and pulling his hair at this point, trying to focus on the fact that I was so close to meeting my baby. The midwife commented that she could see lots of dark hair. It didn't take much for the head to slide out; it was such a relief to hear the midwife say, 'The head's out', and Stuart was saying, 'It really is, I can see it'. She was born at 2.16 p.m., only five minutes after the waters had been broken. The midwife put the baby straight on to my tummy and covered her in a towel. She gave a brief cry and then settled down. The feeling of having her there was just awesome.

I look back on Iona's birth very fondly. It was perfect; just as I'd planned. Having a positive attitude and learning to relax had such an effect on the whole experience. Fourth time round I feel like I'm finally getting the hang of this whole labour thing!

Deborah, mother of Owen (aged ten), Betty (six) Esther (four) and Iona (eighteen months)

CHAPTER ELEVEN

'*Are we there yet?*' — how do you know you are in labour?

Aᴘᴜᴅᴅʟᴇ ᴏɴ ᴛʜᴇ ꜱᴜᴘᴇʀᴍᴀʀᴋᴇᴛ floor, an extra head appear-ing in the middle of the board meeting or a week of contractions – how will you know this is IT?

The first signs that you might not have long to wait are not necessarily the standard textbook ones. You might notice that your baby is quietening down; no longer booting that cup of decaf perched on your bump. Your midwife might tell you your baby has 'dropped' (i.e. the head has engaged in your pelvis). All good stuff, but first babies engage and disengage frequently, so don't uncork the champagne just yet!

Once your baby drops, she leaves a space between your womb and diaphragm for the occasional puff of air. (Remem-ber being able to breathe?) Now you might get that sudden burst of energy – the 'nesting instinct' – which drives you to spring-clean your home. Weirdly enough, some women do find that the minute their home feels ready, they give birth. Unfortunately though, you do need lots of energy for labour; so perhaps retiling the bathroom should wait. Go out for some retail therapy instead, to stock up on champagne and indulge yourself.

Feelings

As your time nears, you might feel no longer able to imagine the reality of a new baby. It's also normal to feel incredibly sensitive just prior to the birth. You're probably finding it hard to concentrate on anything as well. Keep practising your breathing and relaxation routines, and make time for long aromatherapy sessions in the bathroom.

Going into labour any time after thirty-seven weeks is counted as 'on time'; indeed, pregnancies can last up to forty-two weeks and beyond. If your periods are irregular, it might be harder to decide when you conceived, although an ultrasound before thirteen weeks can help. If you are at or past your due date, find things to occupy yourself which are not tiring, and have relaxing baths. You might want to put a message on your ansaphone saying the baby has not yet arrived, and all is well, as believe me, twenty conversations a day as to whether 'anything has happened yet' can get pretty tedious!

Signs of Labour

There are only three real signs that labour has started or is imminent, and these can occur in any order or combination:

- ✿ A 'show'
- ✿ Waters breaking
- ✿ Contractions

A 'show'

As your cervix starts to soften or 'ripen', it opens slightly, and the mucus plug that has formed a barrier between your uterus and vagina during pregnancy can appear. This 'show' looks like heavy discharge and it may have streaks of blood. You might not notice it, as vaginal discharge does get heavier anyway in the time leading up to labour. Sometimes the plug stays in till labour is established, but it can appear up to two weeks before baby arrives. Let your midwife know you've had a show, but there is no need to do anything else. Try to rest, so you are not overtired when it starts for real, but also keep your brain busy and occupied with something else, so you are not focusing on the labour all the time, otherwise you will get very tense and overwrought. A long walk might help the baby settle down into your pelvis.

Try to avoid the temptation to go into hospital 'just to check' if all that has happened so far is the show; if you go in too early, you may well slow everything down and then be offered all sorts of interventions to speed things up. Phone the hospital and talk it through, if you are feeling anxious.

Waters breaking

'Premature rupture of the membranes' happens to very few women, although everyone dreads that sudden gush in the super-market. Even that fabled gush is really only about a teacupful, though yes, it does look like gallons when lying in the pet food aisle. Usually it's the forewaters which go; this is the fluid lying just in front of the baby's head (if your baby is head down). You might even be unsure, so the hospital can check whether a really wet discharge is amniotic fluid. Check the colour; if it's clear you're OK, but if it's stained brown or green, it could mean your baby is in distress.

The most crucial factor is the way baby is lying. If she is still very high, is breech or transverse (see p. 128), there is the possibility that a loop of cord could slip down beneath her head and either become trapped or, worse still, slip out into your vagina. You must get to hospital straight away if your waters go and your baby is not head down.

Eighty-five per cent of women go into labour spontaneously within twenty-four hours of their waters breaking. In the meantime, the baby is still cushioned as fresh amniotic fluid is created all the time. Again, don't sit waiting! Do other things. Take your temperature regularly to check that you are not getting an infection. Be careful about cleanliness when you go to the toilet – wipe yourself away from your vagina.

Don't have penetrative sex. And don't forget to continue to eat and drink; labour is not good on an empty stomach.

Recipe: the perfect meal when you are sitting and waiting to go into labour

Boil some brown rice; while this is cooking, sauté sliced courgettes and mushrooms in olive oil with plenty of fresh rosemary. Meanwhile toast a tray of cashew nuts or almonds in the oven until brown.

When ready, drain the rice, put back on the stove and stir in the vegetables together with a pot of cottage cheese. Lastly, stir in the roasted nuts. Eat when the cheese has melted.

The brown rice gives you slow-release energy, the cheese is full of calcium and protein, rosemary is said to be calming and the nuts contain zinc – nature's fatigue fighter. And it tastes delicious too!

Contractions

Your uterus has been contracting regularly since before the day you were born, limbering up for this time. You only become aware of these sensations now because there is a baby in the way. It's brilliant, really – if only the rest of our muscles would keep themselves toned like this, there would be no need for gyms! Some of these contractions could feel painful, but calling them 'false' labour is a bit negative; they're signs that your cervix is beginning to soften and thin out ready for your baby to be born and, as such, are not wasted.

Practice contractions come and go, but won't increase in strength, and if you change your situation – go for a walk or take a bath, for instance, they will stop. During labour, contractions begin coming at regular intervals and occur increasingly closer together. You can't usually stop established labour, though if you go into hospital too early, even 'real' contractions can stop as adrenaline kicks in (see p. 107).

Although you might immediately know that 'this is IT', most women get a gentle lead-in to labour. In the beginning, contractions can feel like cramping, like painful gas in the intestines or like a regular lower-back pain. First-time nerves make you acutely conscious of every twinge, and many women race into hospital clutching their suitcases, when they misinterpret their practice (Braxton Hicks) contractions. If they are long, erratic and if they go away when you change position, they are probably Braxton Hicks. If they are short, regular and getting stronger, it is probably the real thing. Also, during a 'real' contraction you will not be able to do anything else – e.g. if you phone the midwife to talk about it you won't be able to continue to talk if a contraction arrives. If you are getting lots of Braxton Hicks, it could be sign that you need to rest more.

It's bad news to sit waiting eagerly for that first 'real' contraction, as you will be tired out by the time your energy is actually needed. So keep busy, relax and let things happen. Your body will let you know when you really need to concentrate.

What to Do and When

You should inform your midwife if:

* ✿ you have a show
* ✿ your waters break
* ✿ you think labour has started
* ✿ you are having regular contractions that don't stop – say, every ten minutes

You should go to the hospital when:

* ✿ you no longer feel comfortable at home
* ✿ your waters break early or with a baby that is not engaged
* ✿ contractions are stronger and more definite – say five minutes apart; though go sooner if you have a long journey
* ✿ you are bleeding
* ✿ labour starts before thirty-seven weeks

Going Overdue

Forty-two per cent of women are still pregnant on their due date, while 26 per cent are still pregnant seven days later. The World Health Organisation defines term pregnancy as thirty-seven to forty-two weeks after the last monthly period.

There is quite a lot of controversy over what should happen if you go beyond your expected due date, but NICE (the National Institute for Health and Clinical Excellence) suggest induction somewhere between forty-one and forty-two weeks of pregnancy, with the exact timing taking into account your own preferences and local circumstances. Remember, though, that the research is not clear-cut and it is safer for your baby to be late rather than early.

If you are over, keep an eye on your baby's movements: if she is moving well, then all is probably fine; if she quietens down, it might be a sign that you are about to go into labour (but if she is quiet for long periods, do get checked out).

Artificial induction — what's involved?

There are basically four ways to induce birth artificially, and you might be offered any or all of them.

✿ Your midwife can do a 'stretch and sweep' where she 'sweeps' the membranes just inside the cervix with her finger. Your cervix needs to be ripe for this to be possible.

✿ A prostaglandin pessary can be inserted in your vagina to help soften the cervix. This may start labour on its own – you may need more than one, but sometimes they won't work at all.

✿ The next stage is to break your waters – this is only possible if the cervix is already slightly open. The contractions may be more intense when they start, which might mean you going down the route of using painkillers, etc.

✿ The final option is a syntocinon drip in your arm (artificial oxytocin) which will produce strong contractions. You and your baby will then need continuous monitoring, making it much harder (though not impossible) for you to remain upright and move around. You may also need extra pain relief to cope with the contractions.

While the first two methods can get things going and you can have a perfectly normal birth thereafter, if they don't work, the chances are that having decided that induction is the way to go you will then be into other scenarios like breaking waters and/or syntocinon drips. And thus begins the cascade of interventions (see p. 92).

Alternatively, you can choose to wait and your baby's heartbeat can be checked regularly to check everything is OK.

Inducing labour – self-help methods

You might be able to get labour going yourself without the need for hospital help, although any attempts will probably only work if your baby is good and ready to come. And some won't work at all. Some people swear by really hot curries, others by drinking castor oil. Both these methods would probably only work (if at all) by stimulating the bowel, the idea being that given its proximity to the cervix, it might nudge it into action. On the other hand, it might just give you the runs.

And what about sex, I hear you ask? Have you heard that sexual intercourse, masturbation or nipple stimulation can help induce labour? Well it might be the last thing on your mind as you begin to resemble a beached whale, but all these activities do, in fact, seem to help. Oxytocin, which is the hormone of lurve, and which is released during orgasm and even in the build-up to orgasm, is also the hormone responsible for contractions. And it is also thought that the penis 'nudges' the cervix into action.

There is an argument too that semen is full of prostaglandins, which, if you remember, are used in synthetic form to induce labour to soften the neck of your cervix. But, in fact, this is apparently more effective still if taken orally! (And while you mentally digest *that* little snippet of information, consider whether this is really proof that there is a God and that he is male?)

If semen is to trigger labour through prostaglandins, then it is probably better if it sits in a pool around your cervix, so lie on your back immediately after intercourse with your knees up. (Yes, I know it is undignified, but it's a bit late to be thinking about that now.) So have a go and see what happens. At least it will take your mind off the baby for three, thirty or however many minutes you need. Of course, it could just trigger false labour, but if your body is ready, hopefully the contractions will continue.

A parent's story

In my first pregnancy, one of my big fears was of travelling to hospital in the back of the car trying to be comfortable through contractions. I understood from NCT classes why it was not a great idea to go in too early, but at the same time, I dreaded the idea of being in established labour, immobilised by a seat belt, during a long and bumpy journey. I was also completely terrified of not knowing I was in labour and suddenly giving birth on the kitchen floor.

However, towards the end of that pregnancy, I developed pre-eclampsia, and in the course of one of my check-ups, I was admitted and induced, so labour started and finished in hospital – no car journey, after all. I also never experienced the natural onset of labour with natural contractions, as we used an epidural throughout.

Second birth, I was booked for a home birth, but was told that if I went into labour before thirty-seven weeks, I'd have to go in to hospital. Again, I worried – how would I know that I was in labour, and what about travelling in the car and dealing with contractions? Especially as a second birth would probably be quicker.

I ended up monitoring every little sensation, and the slightest tweak convinced me that this was it! One night, at thirty-four weeks pregnant, I started having Braxton Hicks. I couldn't sleep with them, and started timing them – thirty seconds, every five minutes. With nothing else to do, I lay there waiting for the next one, getting tense and anxious. Eventually, I got into a warm bath, but the contractions carried on.

At 2 a.m., I woke my husband and we rang my dad to get him to babysit. Off we toddled to the hospital, only to be told that the contractions were indeed Braxton Hicks. We drove home again, everyone exhausted from the disturbed night (apart from my toddler, who was raring to go).

At forty-one weeks exactly, having just put Alexander to bed, I had to rush to the loo. Five minutes later, I rushed off again, and again five minutes later. I then realised: oh hang on, this really is it! Sure enough Charlie was born six hours later – at home.

So although it sounds trite, I will say that for me, real contractions left no doubt that it was actually happening. With the Braxton Hicks, I should have done something completely different to take my mind off them, and they would probably have stopped. It was only because I was so focused on them that I became convinced something was happening. But real contractions just don't let you do anything else!

Clare, mother of Alexander (aged four) and Charlie (two and a half)

CHAPTER TWELVE

Coming to terms with the birth you actually had

S O FAR, WE HAVE LOOKED at everything you can do to have the best birth possible. Of course, what actually happens can be quite different, and it is important to acknowledge that there are many women who want to have a natural birth, but who end up with numerous interventions despite all their good intentions.

A 'good' birth is one that leaves you feeling satisfied, not traumatised, in shock or feeling guilty or anxious, and many women do experience such negative emotions for years afterwards. A good birth does not necessarily mean a natural one. It can mean Caesarean, it can mean pain and fear, but what is important is that you feel safe and nurtured throughout, that you understand what is going on at the time and that afterwards you understand what happened and why.

One study looked at a sample of women who had had epidurals, to examine their experiences of birth. What the study found was that those women who felt free of pressure to have an epidural (but still had one) were more likely to feel positive about the birth than those who had been pressurised into having one. (About 60 per cent of women who have epidurals do so for their partner, to alleviate *his* fears.) So here we have two groups of women for whom the actual procedure and outcome were the same, but whose feelings were different. And this was about *control*: if the women felt in control of that choice, they experienced the epidural as liberating.

So it is not necessarily about having the 'perfect birth', but about being happy with what you did have, and part of the time on your babymoon might be well spent going over the birth with your midwife and really understanding what happened and why.

Caesarean

Some women have elective Caesareans because they already know during pregnancy that their baby cannot be born vaginally (for example, with a low-lying placenta or because of particular health problems for mother or baby); this is still a major operation to recover from, but hopefully, if this was your experience, you would at least have been mentally prepared for the event and in control throughout. In these cases, the recovery should be purely physical, but there may well also be a part of you experiencing regret, and you may wish to talk to the midwives and obstetricians about the likelihood of you having a vaginal birth next time round.

An emergency Caesarean is when the need arises midway though labour. Women who experience this say it was almost the worst possible outcome – both physically and mentally exhausting, in terms of having all those contractions, coping with labour, perhaps even pushing as well, then having the Caesarean right at the end. (However, it is worth mentioning here that this is better for the baby than an elective Caesarean, as experiencing contractions and the hormones of labour primes him for the world, making it less likely he will have breathing difficulties at birth, for instance.) There is no doubt that this is a huge event to recover from, and you probably will need to talk it through with your midwives.

Another scenario is that of the woman who is advised to have a Caesarean during pregnancy, decides to attempt a vaginal birth, but ends up with an emergency C-section, after all. Despite the exhaustion and disappointment, they may feel satisfied because they know that they tried – otherwise, they might always have wondered if it would have worked out, after all.

The emergency Caesarean is frightening and can be traumatic. You may well have felt out of control. You will need lots of rest and several opportunities to talk it through with staff; even though you will probably be offered the chance to discuss it straight afterwards, remember that if you feel you need to, you can go back later and talk it through again, when you can absorb it all.

Recovering from a Caesarean section

A C-section is major abdominal surgery and often comes on top of the physical exertion of labour. Immediately afterwards, you will feel a lot of discomfort – apart from the after effects of birth which you share with all new mothers, you'll also have an incision to deal with and, possibly, the effects of anaesthesia. You will be given painkillers for the incision – do take these for as long as you need them; they will not harm your baby. The cut can make it difficult to move around, get comfortable or even cough or laugh. You can support the wound by holding a pillow over your stomach, and wearing loose clothing and huge knickers (see p. 136) can help. You will still need sanitary towels as you will bleed lochia from your vagina, just as if you had a vaginal delivery (see p. 183). Wash and dry your wound carefully every day and check for signs of any infection – discharge, increased tenderness or redness. It's fine to have a shower or bath. It's also worth drinking lots and eating fibre-rich foods to help prevent constipation. Sip peppermint essence in water to avoid the pain of trapped wind which is often common after surgery.

It can take anything from one month to two years to recover fully physically, though the average is about six months. However, the mental recovery can be more difficult. If the Caesarean was unplanned, there can be all sorts of feelings, ranging from a sense of shock, through to feelings of failure and grief, even if both you and the baby are physically fine. Some women feel fine about it immediately afterwards, getting caught up in the excitement and novelty of looking after a baby, but the reaction can hit them many months later. You may find it useful to talk to other women in the same situation; for many women it's also helpful to discuss why a Caesarean was needed with their midwife and obstetrician. It's OK to make an appointment to do this even some time after the event.

It is also useful to know that most women can and do go on to have a vaginal delivery after a Caesarean. In fact, it is so common that it is known by its acronym – VBAC.

Short Labour

A quick labour is not necessarily a good thing. It can be very intense, leaving you in shock, and it may well be stressful for the baby, as well. Although I have said we should not clock watch, as a very average guide, the best sort of labour is twelve to twenty-four hours long for first babies and three to twenty-four hours for subsequent babies. These time scales give you opportunities to adjust, to develop coping strategies, to mobilise the hormones of labour and, basically, to prepare for the delivery.

Friends may well tell you how lucky you were to get it all over and done with so quickly, when in fact you feel numb, in shock, traumatised! It's OK to feel like this – you will have been through a very rushed and hectic experience. You may well need lots of support.

Instrumental Delivery

Perhaps you had an instrumental delivery, using ventouse or forceps? Again, you may need to talk about why this happened, and possibly more than once.

Episiotomy

It is possible to give birth without any need for stitches, but some
women will need stitches due to tearing, while others need them
due to an episiotomy. There can be trauma from stitching for
some time afterwards, particularly if the person doing it is not
skilled. If your stitches are uncomfortable afterwards, go to your
GP and insist he or she sorts it out. Some women go through
months, even years, of painful intercourse due to poor stitching.

Don't Be a Martyr

Some women plough on with feelings of distress and trauma after
their births, in the belief that they should be grateful for having
their baby alive and well. But suppressing or ignoring your feelings will not make them go away, and you will need to find a way
to process them.

This is probably why many women will recount their birth stories in all their gory detail to anyone who will listen, especially the
newly pregnant. It is not about shocking the mother-to-be; it is
just that pressing need to tell all. Getting it out of your system is
really important, but spare the poor innocents. This is the time to

talk to your friends who have given birth before, and while your midwife is still visiting you at home, remember to ask her the endless questions about things you did not understand.

You can also ask for a copy of your hospital records by writing to the local director of midwifery, and you can then make an appointment to meet with a midwife and talk these through.

(See Resources, p. 231, for information on where to find a listening ear.)

A parent's story

The birth of my first child was traumatic and I was left with feelings of failure and fear. When I became pregnant the second time, I was willing to try anything, as I was terrified of giving birth again.

I had a complicated and stressful pregnancy: I contracted pneumonia at seventeen weeks, which resulted in a deep-vein thrombosis, and I developed obstetric cholestasis [where pregnancy hormones adversely affect the liver – the main symptom being severe itching] at thirty-four weeks, meaning I had constant medical attention for the rest of the pregnancy. On top of this, I had recently lost my mum to cancer, and during my pregnancy, my father had a heart attack and my sister was taken ill abroad and had to be flown home. Needless to say, I was a very stressed mum!

I started listening to a hypnotherapy CD at thirty-two weeks and found, within a week or so, that I was much calmer and feeling optimistic about the impending birth. It seemed everyone around me was doing the worrying for me. I was induced at thirty-eight weeks; again, this was not straightforward as they started the induction, then had to stop me for three days, as they had no room for me on the delivery suite.

In spite of all this, the birth itself was great. I was calm and relaxed throughout, other than an initial panic, when the midwife insisted I be constantly monitored, as it meant I would have to lie flat and still for the remainder of the birth. However, my wonderful husband brought me back by getting me to listen to the relaxation part of the CD. From that point on, it was amazing. I initially stopped the contractions to allow myself to get into the right 'zone' (much to the shock of my midwife), then I started them again. Yet I was calm, still and in control. In fact, my husband sat and read a book for several hours until I was ready to push. I felt elated after the birth and full of energy. I was on such a high. I just wanted to do it again – which, in contrast to my feelings of failure and fear with my first child, was amazing.

Victoria, mother of Thomas (aged four) and Samuel (one)

PART THREE

~

Welcome to Your Babymoon

Welcome to your babymoon! I wonder if the birth was what you expected? And how about your baby – does she look anything like you imagined?

After all that build-up, your special time is finally here, and this section of the book will guide you through it. We will start by looking at how your babymoon is likely to begin, which means, of course, thinking about feeding your baby, as well as taking care of both yourself and your baby in very practical ways in those early days of recovery. We will also explore some good strategies to soothe your baby and help her adjust to this new, strange world.

~

CHAPTER THIRTEEN

Things will never be the same again . . .

No MATTER HOW MANY TIMES people tell you that life will never be the same again, you can't really understand this until you look your first baby in the eye and realise that here is a new human being, someone who grew inside you and who will now always be part of you.

If you could bottle the atmosphere in the room just after a birth, you would make a fortune. That heady mixture of relief, powerful hormones and emotions as people welcome a new and unique human being . . . Savour the moment. It will never come again.

It was like being on drugs after Ailsha was born. All my senses felt heightened; I was acutely aware of everything around me, yet at the same time, nothing really mattered except Ailsha. I couldn't take my eyes off her. She was the most beautiful person I had ever seen. It was weird to think that she had been inside me – and she looked so large and so complete! How did I ever give birth to her? At that point, I almost couldn't remember . . .

Jo

Hello Baby

If birth has been straightforward and you have managed to avoid any opiates, you and your baby will be alert and ready to get to know each other, simply gazing into one another's eyes. Your baby will be staring at you, drinking in his first sight of the person whose voice is so familiar. He will also be fascinated by your partner, whose voice he also recognises.

The sound of your voice

Your baby has been listening to your voice over the last few months, but it has sounded different, because he has heard it carried through your body rather than on airwaves, as we normally hear other voices. This is similar to how you hear your own voice, the sound being transmitted through the bones of your skull. So that slightly distorted version of your voice that you are used to hearing, is almost an exact match for your baby's perception of it.

Take your time

There are many special and personal ways in which to welcome your baby into the world. Perhaps you might ask if everyone could leave the room and let you and your partner welcome your baby to the world by yourselves, once they are satisfied that both mother and baby are well. Maybe you would like to say your baby's chosen name to him, or try it out on your own and check that it is right for this baby. (For more on choosing a name, see p. 222–3.)

Whatever you decide to do, imagine you are retreating into your 'cave' for a bit, so you can absorb all that has happened to you. Take time to do this, rather than being rushed off to the postnatal ward, where you will be surrounded by strangers.

In many cultures, the newborn baby is not yet seen as a complete person, but a spirit who only slowly becomes fully human. This might sound a bit daft, but you may get the sense when you meet your baby for the first time, that here is an old and wise spirit. Maybe it is the way he stares intently at you? Or that slightly wrinkled appearance? But your baby will stare at you as if he already knows something about you – and in these first moments, it can feel like something quite profound.

Focusing in

Newborn babies are primed to look out for and focus on faces. Their eyes are relatively bigger in their face than an adult's, and their pupils are more dilated. Dilated pupils not only allow us to take in more light, they also signal attraction. Your baby's eyes are signalling to you, 'Love me!'

The first touch

Usually, your baby will be delivered on to your tummy (although you might have requested this, just to make sure – see p. 133). After that, you will probably instinctively draw your baby up to your chest, cradling him to one side close to your breast. You will then be drawn to touch him, touching his fingers, hands, arms, down his legs and across his trunk. All mothers seem instinctively to follow a similar pattern. That is why being left to do what feels natural is the best thing for you and your baby – you will do what feels just right at that moment in time.

I felt unreal. I stared into Ben's eyes and it was as if we already knew each other. He certainly seemed to know me; he stared right back, and it was as if he was saying, oh you again! I found I was counting his fingers and toes, which was some-thing I had heard women do, and had thought it was silly, but now I felt a compulsion to check that he was all there, com-plete. And of course, he was – he was perfect.

KAREN

Your partner's feelings after the birth

We have talked quite a bit about how you might feel and your need for a babymoon. But your partner is also going through a major life transition – he is becoming a father. He is going to need time to adjust too.

Many men say how disconcerting it is witnessing and participating in the birth of their child in hospital (and perhaps even being traumatised by unfolding events), then being sent home afterwards, having to leave partner and baby behind. They are suddenly back in the 'normal' world, and it is almost as if nothing has happened.

Surely men need a babymoon too? In fact, in Sweden, the country with arguably the best maternity and paternity leave in the world, the whole family recovers from the birth in a 'postnatal hotel', staffed by midwives and nursing assistants. (Mother and baby are moved there after delivery and the father is also welcome to stay; Mum, Dad and baby spending quality time together after the birth – doesn't that sound blissful?)

But does your partner need the same sort of things from a babymoon as you do? I don't think so. I believe he'll need time to adjust to his new role, but I think his feelings are quite different. Instead of being totally absorbed by the baby, as you will be, he will be preoccupied with his family. At some deep level, men tend to see their role as protector and nurturer of the whole family unit.

Although babies are generally quite alert for the first hour or so after birth, your baby may well then sleep for long periods during the first day. Not surprising, really, as birth is pretty tiring. And although you may feel worn out, you will probably also be feeling 'high' and unable to sleep. You might find yourself spending hours just watching your baby – at last you know what he looks like!

> *My dad had brought in a bottle of champagne, and they opened it once they came into the room to meet Daniel. I took a little sip, but I was so high, I didn't really need it. What I really wanted was a cup of tea and some hot buttered toast! Luckily, the midwives were able to get that for me, even at 3 a.m., and I have never tasted better tea and toast since.*
>
> ABIGAIL

All in all, this is the time to rest, recuperate and cuddle. Tuck up in bed together, if you can; if you are in hospital you can ask the midwife to tuck the bedclothes in around both of you, and to show you how to feed lying down. You and your baby need to be close, to get to know each other and to bond.

Getting Your Babymoon Started

You and your partner should by now have agreed on your ideal babymoon together, so how it looks will be unique to you. If you already have children, you can involve them in the planning, perhaps with some special babymoon treats organised just for them: friends or relatives taking them out for the day for a special excursion, for example. You can also talk about some whole-family time, snuggling down to watch favourite films.

You may choose to have someone else to stay to help; your mum (or his) might have volunteered to help out, for instance, and you may feel that this would be a good thing. But you'll both need to think about who is going to be helpful and who is going to hinder? Who is likely to roll their sleeves up and be a real practical help? And who will expect to be waited on and enter-tained? As long as all agree that this is a protected time, where you spend it and with whom, is down to you.

I do suggest you limit visits to the people who are likely to be really helpful and don't overestimate how many visitors you can cope with. The baby is not going to go away, but this special time will be over before you know where you are. You can put a notice on the door saying, 'Please do not disturb – family resting' to dis-courage people from 'popping in' and then staying the whole afternoon.

Kirsty's babymoon cake

After the birth of my second child, I found that I was consistently underestimating the amount I needed to eat to recover from the birth and look after both my new baby and older child. I found I needed to eat practically every hour to avoid feeling wobbly. A friend gave me a cake recipe, which was passed on to her from a distant aunt, and it really seemed to hit the spot. It's a simple recipe (even my husband could make it), and forgiving enough that it could cope if I muddled up the ingredients or overcooked it. It's even good enough to offer to guests, and can be boosted with a chunk of cheese or a banana for a more substantial snack. It keeps indefinitely and can be frozen. Nowadays, I think of it as my Babymoon Cake and I make it as a gift to take to friends who have just given birth:

300ml (½ pint) milk
275g (10 oz) sugar (any combination of brown or white sugar, syrup, treacle, honey, molasses or malt extract)
110g (4 oz) butter or margarine
200g (7 oz) dried fruit (whatever you've got in the house)

350g (12 oz) self-raising flour
1 teaspoon baking powder
1–2 teaspoons spice (ginger, cinnamon, nutmeg – again, whatever you can find)
1 beaten egg

Put the milk, sugar, butter and fruit in a large pan and bring to the boil for 1 minute. Remove from the heat and add the flour, baking powder and spice. Mix well and add the beaten egg.

Pour into a lined 450g (1lb) loaf tin or 20cm (8in) round tin and bake at 170°C (325°F) for approximately 1 hour or until a skewer comes out clean.

Your babymoon space

Ideally, you will want some inner sanctuary to snuggle down with your baby, and so you will probably want to spend at least the first fortnight in your bedroom, if not your bed. This might sound really lazy, but just ask your mum or your granny – bed rest in hospital was probably mandatory for them.

You may or may not feel that you want to be in your bedroom for the entire babymoon period, so you could either start in the bedroom and move out later on or you could make another part of the house into a cosy babymoon space. Your living room could work, for example – although this means you and your partner will have to be even stricter about banning guests from the house for the duration of the babymoon period.

STUFF TO PUT IN YOUR BABYMOON SPACE
- CD player and radio (you probably won't want an MP3 player, as this will cut you off from your baby).
- Plenty of pillows and cushions.
- Magazines.

- ❂ If you can fit them in, a TV and DVD player – time to catch up on all those films you've recorded (or rent out ones you've always fancied watching; see Resources, p. 232).
- ❂ Sports bottles of water.
- ❂ Changing mat, nappies, wipes, etc. for the baby (see p. 67).
- ❂ Toiletries for pampering (maybe you got some at your baby shower? – see p. 71); face creams, body lotion, hand and foot cream, lip salve and the like will help to freshen you up whenever you feel a bit jaded.
- ❂ If you are having a summer baby you may need a fan (but it will be lovely to throw the windows open too); for a winter baby, an extra heater is useful in case the room gets chilly, or in case you open the window for fresh air and need to heat the space.
- ❂ A pile of takeaway menus (from places that deliver).
- ❂ A large fruit bowl (any visitors who want to bring something can be asked to top it up).

I would also suggest that you leave the phone and laptop out of your special space, so that interactions with the outside world are kept to a minimum. When you feel like phoning someone, get your partner to bring the phone to you and take it away again afterwards. Better still, send them a text, then switch your phone off again. You could always change your ansaphone message to give out the good news.

A list of your favourite snacks and recipes pinned up in the kitchen where everyone can see it is also a great idea!

We had had a tough time after the birth of our first child, who was premature, and we really needed the space to settle as a new family. We had lots of visitors, however, who wanted to sit and coo over the baby and brought neatly wrapped gifts of pretty baby clothes (which were far too big). But one visitor took a very different approach: she brought a raw chicken, put it in the oven, took my shopping list to the supermarket, came back, unpacked the shopping, took the chicken out of the oven and left. We ate that hot chicken practically with our bare fingers, with bread and butter and a bag of salad. I've never forgotten the value of that simple practical gift over all the more traditional presents.

KIRSTY

(See also Kirsty's babymoon cake recipe, p. 164.)

CHAPTER FOURTEEN

Getting your babymoon off to a brilliant start with breastfeeding

Now BEGINS THE BUSINESS OF looking after your new baby. So let's start by thinking about feeding. Breastfeeding is as natural as breathing: it's entirely under the influence of your hormones and your baby's instincts, yet it can still seem daunting at first. Knowing what is supposed to happen helps. But, more importantly, making the time and space to get it established is crucial. Hence your babymoon.

Why breastfeed?

❀ Breast milk is more than just nutrition; it is a protective, living fluid. Your baby's immune system will take up to a year to develop fully, and in the meantime she receives your own antibodies through your milk.

❀ Breastfeeding develops your baby's jaw in preparation for chewing and also talking.

- The pauses and eye contact, the interaction that takes place when you are breastfeeding, all prepare her for conversing later.
- Your baby's teeth will be better aligned than they would if she is bottle-fed.
- Your baby will taste the food you eat, thus preparing her to join the family at mealtimes.
- Breast milk is so perfectly digestible that even nappies will smell sweet!
- Breastfeeding is intimate and enjoyable, a way of bringing you closer together. What more could a baby want?

The Hormone Continuum

Your body has nurtured your baby throughout pregnancy, and after the birth your breasts are perfectly designed to take over from the placenta in nurturing her. As with pregnancy, breast-feeding is controlled by hormones, to keep the amount of milk at exactly the right level to nourish your baby, and to let it out just when your baby wants it.

If you had a normal birth, you'll be hormonally ready for breastfeeding (see pp. 93–4), your baby will be active and alert and she may well latch on to your breast unaided. Babies instinctually know how to breastfeed, so if you lie back with your baby on top of you, so you are both 'skin to skin', you may see her 'rooting' for the breast – bobbing her head up and down with her mouth wide open.

Prolactin

This is the hormone in charge of producing milk during your babymoon. During pregnancy, it gets your breasts to develop milk-producing cells and to make a small amount of milk, which you may have noticed leaking from your breasts from about week twenty, though volume is kept low by progesterone – another pregnancy hormone. This early, low-volume milk is called colostrum and it's what your baby will get at birth. A few days after birth, progesterone levels fall, allowing milk production to increase; this stage is referred to as your milk 'coming in'. From this point onwards, the milk changes gradually from colostrum to mature milk.

Colostrum is fantastic stuff: high in antibodies and protein, it also has a laxative effect to help your baby clear meconium (sticky black poo) from her intestines.

Whenever your baby stimulates your nipples you release prolactin, which tells your body to create more milk. Nature assumes that you and your baby are novices, so the prolactin will keep the milk supply reasonably high for the first six weeks, i.e. during your babymoon. After this time, your body knows how much your baby needs, the prolactin falls away and, from now on, your milk supply is maintained by your baby emptying the breast. And what's so interesting is that this time frame of forty days is just what traditional societies specify as the ideal baby-moon length.

However, if milk is not removed from the breasts, prolactin levels fall and milk production will eventually cease. Also, any milk left in the breasts actually contains a substance designed to decrease prolactin levels, so if your baby is not milking the breast effectively, your supply will fall. So during your babymoon, feed your baby as often as possible; you are investing in your milk supply.

At the end of the babymoon period (i.e. six weeks), your milk supply volume is at its peak. It will no longer increase, but what will happen is that its consistency will change, as your baby gets older, so that it will always satisfy her appetite, as well as fulfilling her developmental needs.

Oxytocin

This is the other main hormone involved in breastfeeding, and it is responsible for ejecting milk from the breasts in what's known as the 'let-down' reflex. Muscles high up in your breasts contract, squeezing milk down towards your nipples where your baby can get it. Some women are unaware of this, while others find it a strange, almost tickly feeling, and a few will find it slightly painful. This hormone also helps your uterus to contract, so when you feed your baby in the early days of your babymoon you may feel 'after pains'.

Oxytocin is a more wide-ranging hormone than prolactin in that it can be switched on by different stimuli; feeding your baby raises oxytocin levels, but just holding your baby also works, even thinking about her when she's not there. That's why it's possible to express breast milk without your baby present.

Your baby can get quite a lot of milk from what is 'let down' by oxytocin. However, she also needs to play an active part in empty-ing the breasts, so that she can increase the prolactin levels to produce enough milk for the next feed. Also, as fat is thicker than water, it tends to stick to the inside of the storage cells in the breast, so what drips out of the breast through the let-down reflex contains less fat. This thinner milk which comes before is often referred to as foremilk. If this is all that your baby drinks, she will need to feed more frequently, as she will not be getting the levels of fat she needs to grow. She may also get colicky if she's drinking mostly foremilk, as this passes through the gut quickly and may reach the lower intestine before all the lactose is absorbed, where it ferments and causes discomfort as well as green, explosive nappies!

Therefore, having your baby empty your breasts effectively is very important, not only in building and maintaining the milk supply, but also in extracting the fat-rich hindmilk.

The effects of labour on breastfeeding

❀ If you were given pethidine during labour, especially within a few hours of the birth, it can depress your baby's suckling reflex for several days. This can mean it takes longer for breastfeeding to get established, so in the meantime, have as much skin-to-skin contact as you can, and keep waking her and offering her the breast.

❀ A Caesarean section can also affect your baby's ability to feed in many different ways: the anaesthetic can make your baby drowsy, while milk may be delayed coming in after a planned Caesarean. However, the main issues are usually about finding comfortable positions to feed. It may work best for you to lie back and have your baby directly on top of you, or you might find having her in an underarm hold works well. Lying on your side can also work with help.

❀ An assisted delivery with forceps or ventouse can give your baby a headache, so that being held in certain positions or even suckling could be painful for her. She may need you to experiment with different positions.

Early Feeding

Your babymoon is the time when both you and your baby invest in your milk supply. At first, your baby will feed little and often. Her tiny tummy, which is only the size of a marble, can't hold much. Also, she is learning how to feed and tires quickly, so allow her to latch on and off at will. After the babymoon is over, and your baby is stronger and more alert, feeding will be far less time consuming.

Don't worry too much if your baby doesn't seem interested in food at first, but do spend as much time as you can in skin-to-skin contact, offering her the breast during her brief moments of alertness. Your midwife may suggest waking your baby to feed, as sleepy babies can get lethargic and 'forget' to feed.

Jaundice is common in newborn babies, making them look as if they have a lovely suntan. Breastfeeding as often as possible helps this pass, but again you may need to wake her to feed as jaundice does make babies sleepy (see p. 192).

You will soon come to recognise your baby's hungry signals: she will become restless, her head will turn from side to side, as if looking for something, her mouth will open and her tongue will extend. If she can't find the breast, she will cry, but it's better if you can feed her before she gets to that point as crying is tiring, and she won't feed as effectively.

> ## Victoria's recipe for your babymoon
>
> 'Healthy, easy meals for me included porridge with a mashed-up banana and cinnamon. Oats are supposed to be very good for your milk supply.'
> (See also Victoria's story on pp. 155–6.)

Is She Getting Enough to Eat?

It's easy to become obsessed with your baby's weight, wondering if she is getting enough to eat, but this is only one part of the picture, and it's important to look at the overall pattern. Anyway, sometimes your baby's weight will fluctuate if different scales are used or if your baby did a bowel motion just before being weighed, for example.

What's important is whether your baby is generally alert, healthy and interacting with you. And nappies are also a good indicator of what's going on; you will probably need to change them about six times a day, and they should feel heavier each time. Bowel motions will be bright yellow, sweet smelling and the consistency of scrambled eggs; expect at least one a day in the babymoon period.

How Breastfeeding Works

Have you thought about why it's called 'breastfeeding'? It's because your baby feeds from a mouthful of breast; she doesn't just suck on your nipples. Consider your mouth shape when taking a first bite from a large apple – this is how breastfeeding should look. Your baby should open her mouth wide to take the breast, and even when she's on, her gape should still be wide. Her chin will dig into your breast, but her nose will be relatively clear. (You don't need to worry about keeping her nose clear; it is a perfectly designed shape for breastfeeding.) You may see her jaw quivering, which triggers the let-down, and then you will see it moving steadily and powerfully, maybe even making her ears wiggle up and down; you might hear her swallowing too. Her jaw works together with a rolling action of her tongue to squeeze milk out of the breast.

You need to allow your baby to move her head freely to latch on to the breast, preferably in a way that allows her back, shoulders and head to be in a straight line. This is simply because it's really difficult to swallow if your head is turned sideways or if your chin is sinking down towards your chest – try it yourself and see! In the early days, this might mean you lying back propped up on pillows with your baby lying on top of you so her head is able to access the breast. Or you might want to lie on your side, again with her body facing yours. Roll forward slightly, so you can see what you're doing and so that your breast is hanging forward, and support your head and shoulders with lots of pillows. Your lower arm can extend out and round the top of your baby's head. Use your upper arm to position your baby and draw her on to your lower breast.

Later on, perhaps towards the end of your babymoon, you might want to feed more discreetly or sitting up. If so, hold her body so she is facing your breast, with her nose next to your nipple to begin with. Where your nipples point will decide whether she is lying on her back, looking up at you or being held higher up, so she is facing you, 'tummy to tummy'; but try to imagine a line running from deep inside your breast, through your nipple, into your baby's mouth and out the back of her head – that line should be dead straight for feeding. If you tuck her bottom in close and leave her neck and head relatively clear, you will find this allows her to extend her neck better.

Avoiding Breastfeeding Problems

The majority of breastfeeding problems come from the baby not latching on to your breast in the optimum way. Make sure you ask for help from your midwife in the crucial early days.

Sore nipples

Many women have sensitive nipple skin for the first week after birth. You are also not used to the strong sensation of your baby's feeding action, so it can feel uncomfortable, even painful. There is a difference though, between discomfort from something you are not used to and pain which is warning you that you are damaging your nipples. When your baby latches on, wait for thirty seconds, and if you still feel uncomfortable, take her off and start again. If you are finding it particularly painful, practise relaxation (see p. 49) at the beginning of the feed, then try to latch your baby on when she is just waking up, before she gets really hungry. The most important consideration though, is that when she comes off your breast, your nipples should not look chaffed or distorted. If they do, ask for help attaching her, because your nipples may become damaged if you continue to feed like this.

It's miserable having sore nipples. Nipple skin is very like the skin on your lips – easily cracked and incredibly painful when damaged. If your nipples have become damaged to the extent that the skin is broken, you can use a pure lanolin cream like Lansinoh or Purelan to soothe the pain and to help the cracks heal. Your midwife might also offer a dressing called Gelnet. It is best not to let cracks dry out and form scabs, as these will keep reopening when your baby feeds.

Thrush

Another less common reason for sore nipples is thrush, which can occur if you have had it during pregnancy, are prone to it, or if you or your baby have recently taken antibiotics. Thrush causes severe nipple pain and sometimes deep breast pain; your nipple skin may look lighter than usual and shiny, and your baby may have white flecks in her mouth. Women usually report that the pain continues throughout the feed and between feeds, and ordinary things like taking a shower can be painful as the water touches the nipples.

If you think you have thrush it is important that both you and your baby are treated by your GP, even if your baby shows no symptoms, to avoid cross-infection. Ask a breastfeeding counsellor about current topical applications for thrush.

Signs that your baby has thrush are:

- pulling away and crying while feeding
- white spots in the mouth which look like drops of milk, but which don't go away
- sometimes, thrush on her bottom, which manifests as a nappy rash of paler, shiny skin

Sore breasts

ENGORGEMENT

A few days after the birth, when your milk 'comes in', your breasts may become 'engorged' (hot, swollen and uncomfortable) and it can be hard for your baby to latch on. In fact, your breasts are not full of milk, but are swollen with excess fluid due to an increased blood supply. It will pass within twenty-four hours; but in the meantime, frequently feeding your baby will help. Some women find ice-cold flannels bring relief. Cabbage leaves do seem to help too – especially Savoy cabbages; try holding a chilled leaf against your breast.

Once breastfeeding is established, engorgement usually only happens again if you go too long between feeds or miss feeds, and you can feel this coming on. If you start to feel a bit full, put the baby to your breast or express some milk if your baby is not with you.

BLOCKED DUCTS

Leaving milk in your breast until you feel uncomfortable can lead to blocked ducts. You can feel these as painful lumps, and they can also occur if your bra doesn't fit well or if you have something restricting your milk flow during a feed, such as your hand or your baby's hand pressing against your breast. If you develop a blocked duct, feeding your baby is the best cure, gently massaging the lump towards your nipple while your baby is feeding. It also helps if you can get your baby's chin nearest to the lump when feeding, so if it is on the outer side of your breast, try feeding underarm on that side, for instance.

Mastitis

Blocked ducts or engorgement, if untreated, can lead eventually to mastitis. Milk trapped in the breasts overflows from the ducts into surrounding breast tissue, where the body treats it as a foreign substance and rallies the immune system to fight.

If you are unlucky enough to develop mastitis, you will feel fluey, may have a temperature and your breasts will be sore. Try to rest and drink plenty of fluids. It is important to keep feeding your baby, as stopping breastfeeding will make the problem worse. Usually, if you clear the blocked duct or engorgement, the mastitis will ease.

Your GP may give you antibiotics, but most cases of mastitis are not caused by infection, so antibiotics are purely precautionary; the drugs your GP prescribes will be safe to take while breastfeeding, though antibiotics may upset her tummy, and you need to watch out for thrush – see above. Ask your GP about anti-inflammatory drugs to reduce the inflammation.

Breast abscess

It is important to treat mastitis promptly, as left untreated it could develop into a breast abscess, which would have to be drained surgically. If you can identify why you got mastitis, you can prevent it happening in the future, so talk it through with a breastfeeding counsellor (see Resources, p. 232).

Out and About With Your Breastfed Baby

One of the big fears that new mums have is about breastfeeding in public or in front of other people. While you probably won't find it easy to feed discreetly at first, within a couple of weeks, or certainly by the end of your babymoon, you should be able to feed pretty much automatically, and then it will be easier to go places with your baby. Many shopping centres now have specific spaces for feeding babies, but you can usually feed anywhere once you've mastered the art. Wear a loose top or drape a shawl around both of you, and avoid button-through tops.

What Happens If You Can't Breastfeed?

Hopefully, having the time and space that a babymoon offers will mean that you are able to overcome any breastfeeding difficulties. Remember that you don't have to do this on your own; there are many organisations and people out there who you can call on for help without even moving from your babymoon space (see Resources, p. 232). There is also the option to express your breast milk and feed this to your baby in a bottle; many women have fed their babies exclusively on breast milk without ever having their babies at their breasts. Again, the voluntary organisations can help you with this option.

If, however, despite all your best intentions and efforts, you are not able to breastfeed, please do still pick up the phone and talk to one of the trained counsellors at the other end. They can help you come to terms with not breastfeeding. Despite the negative scare stories in the media, the NCT is not about bullying you into breastfeeding; it is about supporting you in your own parenting choices, and if this includes not breastfeeding, you can be sure that you will find support in this decision as well. Guilt about not breastfeeding is a huge thing; many NCT breastfeeding counsellors have also been through it and come out the other side and would be only too happy to help you get there too.

A parent's story

My second baby had tongue tie and so he had difficulty latching on to the breast. On day three or four, I was still struggling, my milk had come in and I was feeling really weepy. My husband couldn't watch me being upset any more, and wanted to give Ed a bottle, but my mum said, 'No – ring the NCT breastfeeding line'. So I rang, and had a really long chat with the breastfeeding counsellor. She was able, over the phone, to help me get Ed latched on, and we never looked back. It was such a brilliant experience that I decided, later on, that I too would train to be a breastfeeding counsellor.

Frances, mother of Alice (aged ten) and Edward (eight)

~

CHAPTER FIFTEEN

Taking care of yourself

I N THE NEXT CHAPTER, WE will think about the practicalities of caring for your baby, but it is also really important that you take good care of yourself. It's like they say on aeroplanes, 'Put the oxygen mask on yourself first, before helping others'! So here, we'll be talking about using this babymoon time to let yourself recover fully from the birth, nurturing yourself, so you can also nurture your baby.

When to Leave Hospital

There is no exact time when you 'should' leave hospital. If you feel well supported and cared for in hospital, then negotiate to stay there as long as you need to. Having said that, many postnatal wards are noisy, busy places where it is hard to rest, and staff are overstretched, unable to offer the women in their care the full attention they require. So if you feel you would be better off out of there, you can choose to go home.

You should be offered comprehensive postnatal care at home, initially by your community midwife, and thereafter by your health visitor. NICE recognises the importance of good postnatal care and has drawn up clinical guidelines for practitioners, but despite this, in many areas of the UK the cover can be patchy and inadequate (see Resources, p. 232). Make sure you have your community midwife's phone number and ring her if you need help or advice.

'How Do I Look?'

Forget looking glamorous after giving birth! That slightly glowing look with make-up still intact that you see in films? Just another hideous plot to make new mums feel inadequate. You may have bloodshot eyes from pushing, you'll look tired and dishevelled and it can come as a shock to realise that after you've given birth, you still look pregnant. Your bump will look like a half-deflated football, similar in size to six months' gestation. Not a pleasant sight, but rest assured that it will shrink and become firmer as the days pass. (Unfortunately, while this is happening you could experience 'after pains', as your uterus contracts back – see p. 171.)

It is quite normal to sweat a lot after the birth; your body will need to get rid of the extra fluid you carried during pregnancy. You may also lose some hair in the first week or so as your hormones settle down.

So no longer blooming marvellous, but you guessed that, didn't you? Don't neglect yourself though at this time – looking better can also help you to feel better. Here are a couple of tips:

✿ If you do have friends or relatives popping in to see you in hospital, ask them to bring you some nail varnish and paint your finger- and toenails for you! Choose a light colour, so that any chips won't show so much.
✿ A pot of shimmering face cream will enhance your complexion and help to combat the skin-drying effects of the heat in the postnatal ward.

Bleeding After the Birth

You will bleed after giving birth even if you've had a Caesarean. It is heavier and lasts longer than a period, with large clots over the first few days. This discharge is called lochia. Expect it to eventually turn to a watery pink, then brown, then yellow before it ceases altogether. You should use sanitary towels, not tampons (this is where those granny knickers come in handy – see p. 232).

Bleeding may continue off and on for as long as six weeks, though one to two weeks is normal. (A bit of a bummer, but then you won't have periods for quite some time if you continue to breastfeed exclusively.)

Call your midwife urgently if the bleeding becomes suddenly heavier or bright red, if clots continue after the first couple of days or if it becomes unpleasantly smelly.

Your Perineum

Unless you had an early Caesarean, your perineum will feel sore and bruised. If you are particularly tender, you could sit on a pillow or a rubber ring (see Resources p. 232). Pelvic-floor exercises will stimulate the circulation in that area, promoting healing.

A small tear can take up to ten days to heal, but anything larger may take longer and will probably need stitches. Some midwives prefer not to stitch small tears as they believe they heal better that way. If this is the case, you may need to keep your legs together as much as possible in the early days to let the tear knit, but your midwife will advise you.

If you had an episiotomy (cut), you will definitely have needed stitches. The midwife should check your stitches on every visit and she shouldn't 'discharge' you until she is satisfied they've healed.

Keep any stitches clean and dry, and eat a fibre-rich diet to aid the easy passage of stools. Drink lots, so that your urine is dilute and will not sting. Good hygiene is important to avoid infection, so wash your hands before changing sanitary towels and do change them frequently. Use medical wipes on toilet seats, if you are in hospital, and when wiping yourself with toilet paper, take extra care to wipe front to back only. To keep the whole area clean, stand in the bath and using either a jug or the shower head, spray pointing downwards then pat dry, working front to back. Pouring warm, salty water over the whole area from front to back can be soothing.

The stitches will feel sore as they dry and tighten, but if they still don't feel better after a week to ten days, tell your midwife. In the meantime, a cold compress helps: put some ice cubes in a plastic bag, wrap it in a towel and hold it against your stitches.

The following tips may also help to soothe the area:

- ❧ Soak in a bath with a few drops of lavender oil.
- ❧ Drink raspberry leaf tea to promote healing and help tone your uterus.
- ❧ Arnica – a homeopathic remedy – can help reduce bruising.
- ❧ Infuse calendula or marigold flowers in boiling water, strain and cool and apply to the stitches' area to encourage healing and help ease pain.
- ❧ Use a cold compress with witch hazel to reduce swelling and bruising.

Your Bladder and Bowels

You should need to pee a lot after the first day as your body gets rid of excess fluid. If you don't seem to be passing much water, tell someone in case this is the first sign of infection. Watch out in particular for any burning sensation when you pee, or a lower-back pain, which could indicate a kidney infection.

Passing water while your perineum is tender can be painful; one suggestion is to pour a jug of warm water between your legs as you pee to alleviate any stinging. If you are reluctant to 'let go', try sitting on the toilet within earshot of a running tap.

Then there's your first poo – that psychological fear of pushing while you feel so tender. Fortunately, you may not need to go for a while, as labour usually pushes everything out.

Take your time sitting on the toilet, relax and see if anything happens. Support any stitches or tearing by pressing a clean sanitary towel to your perineum when opening your bowels. If nothing seems to be happening, eat lots of fibre – fruit, whole grains, bran – and drink plenty of water. Try to walk around a little bit to get your circulation moving. If you are feeling gassy, sip some warm water containing a few drops of peppermint essence.

Many women have haemorrhoids (piles) after giving birth. These feel like small lumps around the anus and usually retreat without treatment, but if they are still there at your six-week check up, tell your GP. You need to avoid straining heavily when passing a motion to avoid exacerbating them, so again, plenty of roughage in your diet will help.

Eating For Two

The good news is that you can start eating nearly all the things that were banned before! But consult a health professional before taking any medications, and be aware that you should still avoid those fish that are higher up in the food chain (see p. 271) to protect your baby's brain development. Alcohol does pass into your breast milk, but your body will process it quite quickly, so a good tip is to have a glass of wine during or immediately *after* feeding.

It is true that breastfeeding helps you lose weight, but only if you are careful about what you eat and follow your appetite, i.e. eat when you are hungry and stop when you are full. Nature is very efficient, and it is estimated that you only need an extra 200–500 calories per day when breastfeeding, including about 70g (2oz) extra protein.

You will probably find that breastfeeding makes you starving hungry, so make sure that someone is keeping the larder well stocked with nutritious foods, and don't forget to have that list of nutritious snacks (see p. 124) pinned up in the kitchen, where well-wishers will see it!

Making Your Babymoon Space a Good Place in Which to Recuperate

Hopefully, your space is already organised with everything to hand (see p. 165), but here are some extra treats that you might like to have:

- ❀ Fresh flowers
- ❀ Scented candles
- ❀ Clean bed linen every day or so (ask your partner to change it)
- ❀ A selection of magazines to browse through when baby is sleeping and you are feeling wide awake

You might also like to see if you can organise a home pedicure, manicure or even hairdo.

Don't forget to spend some time practising your relaxation skills and writing in your journal (see pp. 47 and 54). A relaxing aromatherapy bath while Dad cuddles up with baby for a rest himself is also a great idea.

Try not to lie down all day; get up and walk about a bit or, if you are in bed, keep changing position. This will help your circulation, and begin the process of letting your bladder and bowels recover from the delivery. Start gently working your pelvic-floor muscles as soon as you feel able (see p. 215), and sit on your birth ball to work your abs gently.

While the room you are in does need to be warm, aim to open the window and let in fresh air twice a day; this is just as refreshing as going outside. Sit under the window, wrapped up in your dressing gown, sipping a smoothie.

Feelings of Depression

Having a baby is a life-changing experience, and for many new mothers, feeling tearful and depressed is common. You could try pulsatilla (a homeopathic remedy) for when you are feeling weepy or Bach flowers Rescue Remedy for shock after birth.

However, sometimes longer periods of depression, known as postnatal depression (PND), can occur during the first few weeks and months of the baby's life.

PND can have a variety of physical and emotional symptoms, and many women are unaware that they have the condition. It affects about one in ten mothers in the UK, and usually develops in the first four to six weeks after childbirth, though in some cases it may take several months to develop. It can be lonely, distressing and frightening, but be reassured that it's always treatable. It's very important to understand that having PND doesn't mean that you don't love or care for your baby.

Common PND myths

PND is very often misunderstood and many myths surround the condition:

Myth: PND is less severe than other types of depression.
Fact: PND is as serious as other types of depression.
Myth: PND is entirely caused by hormonal changes.
Fact: PND is actually caused by many different factors.
Myth: PND will go away by itself.
Fact: PND is usually only resolved with treatment.

Symptoms of PND usually include one or more of the following:

❀ Low mood for prolonged periods of time (a week or more)
❀ Feeling irritable a lot of the time
❀ Tearfulness
❀ Panic attacks or feeling trapped in your life
❀ Difficulty concentrating
❀ Lack of motivation
❀ Lack of interest in yourself and your new baby

- ✿ Feeling lonely
- ✿ Feeling guilty, rejected or inadequate
- ✿ Feeling overwhelmed
- ✿ Feeling unable to cope
- ✿ Difficulty sleeping
- ✿ Physical signs of tension, such as headaches, stomach pains or blurred vision

If you think that you may have postnatal depression you should see your GP, midwife or health visitor as soon as possible so that a diagnosis can be made, and an appropriate course of treatment undertaken. (See also Resources, p. 232.)

A PARENT'S TIP

Three days after my first child was born, I thought it would be a good idea to go to the supermarket. This was not because we had run out of anything, but rather because my mind was telling me that shopping was a normal thing to do after not being out of the house for a while. However, it became apparent, as my husband and I wandered around the vast neon-lit building in a sort of freaked-out daze, staring at our slightly jaundiced infant, that neither my body nor my emotions, my baby or my husband was ready for the outside world. Goodness knows what we actually bought, but the return home was swift and I was so traumatised by the experience that it was a full seven days before I ventured over the threshold again.

I would recommend to any first-time mothers of newborns that *normal rules do not apply* and to take it ever so easy in the first couple of weeks.

Manda, mother of Tansy (aged five) and Guthrie (two)

~

CHAPTER SIXTEEN

Taking care of your baby

ONE OF THE REASONS FOR such a long babymoon is that it is going to take you quite a while to get the hang of all those baby-care tasks, like changing nappies, keeping him clean and so on. It works much better if you can view these 'chores' as time for you and your baby to get to know each other and to bond. So when changing nappies, you might sing songs, recite nursery rhymes or blow raspberries on his tummy – generally interacting with him and having fun, rather than rushing through whatever you are doing so you can get on with the next thing.

The babymoon is also a good time for your partner to bond with his baby, and what better way than being really involved in baby care from day one, so he also has the opportunity to communicate with the baby and to get to know him? For both of you, slowing down and focusing on your baby without the demands of the outside world really gives you a chance to tune in and learn about this new person and to gain in confidence.

What Your Baby Will Look Like

We all have an idealised image of a baby in our minds, but this is often modelled on one who is several months old, while in reality, newborn babies can look distinctly odd.

After a vaginal birth, his head may look slightly elongated (a bit like an egg), but it will right itself over a few months. Forceps or ventouse will leave bruising and marks as well. His eyes might be swollen, puffy or show broken veins after the birth, but again, this will clear up soon afterwards. Many parents think their babies have sticky-out ears, but that's only because they have such fine hair; the ears will become less noticeable when the hair grows.

It is normal for your baby to have slightly enlarged breasts after birth (boys as well as girls) and for their genitals to be swollen. Girls may also have a vaginal discharge. All of this is due to hormones picked up from you in the womb, and will settle soon after birth.

If your baby was born early or on time, he will probably be covered with a white cream called vernix, which helped protect his skin from the effects of being submerged in water in the womb. This is wondrous stuff, so let it absorb fully into your baby's skin; don't bathe him until it's all gone. If he's born late, the vernix will have worn off, and his skin may look dry and flaky.

Your baby's skin might seem to go through the mill in these early weeks! Up till now he's been in a sterile environment; emerging into the world his skin is the first line of defence against dirt, germs and pollution. It is quite normal, therefore, to get rashes and skin complaints. Some babies get little white spots called 'milk rash' and they clear up with time. Red spots with a yellow centre (more like pimples) are called neonatal urticaria and are a sign that your baby's skin pores are not yet working efficiently; these don't need treatment, but don't be tempted to squeeze them as you will leave scars.

Another common skin reaction on babies' heads is cradle cap, which resembles very large dandruff scales covering your baby's head. It's not actually dandruff though, and has nothing to do with how clean your baby's hair is; it is similar to eczema, if anything. You can brush off loose flakes with a soft hairbrush, but don't pick at it and damage the skin as it may get infected. You can also loosen the flakes with vegetable or olive oil.

Thrush

This is something babies can pick up during birth (see p. 176), or it can develop after a course of antibiotics. It can be seen as white spots in your baby's mouth, and sometimes as a form of nappy rash, where the skin is sore and shiny. Your GP can prescribe a cream for his bottom or drops for his mouth. (See Chapter Fourteen for information about thrush and breastfeeding.)

Be careful about the creams and lotions you use on your baby; use as few as possible to play it safe. A barrier cream is useful in the beginning when you need to clean off meconium (see below), and later on it is good for preventing nappy rash, but don't use it unless your baby's bottom seems to need it. Leave his nappy off for a short time every day to air instead.

Most detergents contain fairly strong chemicals, so you might want to swap to a milder variety for the time being, and leave out the fabric conditioner. Be careful too about chemicals around the house.

Post-birth check-up

If your baby was born in hospital, it is usual to have a check up with a paediatrician before you both leave the hospital. For home births, your GP will normally visit on the first day to do a post-birth check up. The doctor will listen to your baby's heart and lungs, and check his hip joints and reflexes.

THE GUTHRIE TEST

About six to ten days after the birth, your midwife will do a blood test to check for various metabolic disorders; usually she pricks the baby's heel and extracts a few drops of blood, during which your baby may well scream the house down! Some mothers breastfeed through it and say this helps, others leave the room and put a pillow over their heads to muffle the noise . . .

Cord Care

After birth, your baby's umbilical cord will have been clamped with a plastic clip to make sure no blood is lost from it; the midwife will remove this after a few days. Keep the area around the cord clean by wiping it with a damp cotton wool ball. You need to keep the area dry, so you might need to fold the top of the nappy over. The cord stump will dry up and fall off after about a week.

Jaundice

Over half of all babies develop jaundice. This happens when the baby's immature liver has not been able to process bilirubin – a by-product of the breakdown of the excess red blood cells that your baby needed in the womb – fully, and it results in a yellow-ish tinge to the skin. Jaundice occurs around the second or third day, peaks on the third to fifth day, then begins to disappear, and is perfectly normal. The problem is that jaundice can make babies sleepy so they forget to feed, and as colostrum helps your baby expel bilirubin from his bowels, frequent breastfeeding is what's needed.

If jaundice deepens and bilirubin reaches higher levels, your baby may need phototherapy – basically, time under a sun lamp! Breastfeeding will help him recover more quickly, so keep feeding him as often as you can.

Day-to-day Baby Care

Topping and tailing

You don't need to bathe your baby every day, but it is a good idea to 'top and tail' – wash his face and bottom – regularly. As you do this, you can chat and make eye contact, so choose a time when he's alert and ready to interact.

- It's easiest to work on a changing mat on the floor, so that you won't need to worry about your baby rolling off as he gets bigger.
- You want to avoid spreading any infection, so use cotton wool balls and throw them away after use. Simply immerse each one in a bowl of warm water and squeeze it out, so it's just damp when you use it.
- Start by wiping each eye with a separate ball, working from the inner corner outwards.
- Use another ball to wipe around his mouth and nose.
- Finally, take another ball and clean his ears, neck and face, paying attention to neck creases where milk and fluff get trapped.
- Don't put anything like a cotton bud in his ears or nose; just wipe what you can see.
- You can then wash his hands and feet, looking out for sharp fingernails. Babies often scratch themselves with these, so remove any scraggy ends, either with tiny scissors or you could just chew them off.
- Finally you can 'tail': take the nappy off and wash your baby's bottom and genitals, just cleaning what you can see. Don't try to pull back the foreskin or clean inside the vagina. (Girls need to be wiped front to back, to keep poo away from the genitals.) If there is a dirty nappy and you want to start with the 'tailing', change the water before you 'top'.

Bathing

While some babies take to baths well, others really dislike them, so you may have to experiment before you find a way that you can both enjoy. When he's tiny he could probably fit in the sink, but very soon he will need to go in the main bath. A rubber mat might be useful as babies can feel slippery!

Some babies hate being unwrapped as they feel unsupported and unsafe. In this case, you could keep him swaddled in a towel until the last minute, then lower him slowly so he doesn't feel he's falling.

- ❀ Get the room as warm as you can before you start – babies chill quickly. Try to keep the temperature in the room at least at 21°C.
- ❀ Run the bath to body temperature; test it with your elbow – it should feel neither hot nor cold, but neutral. Also, be sure to keep it shallow.
- ❀ Put a squirt of baby bath in the water – you don't need a separate shampoo.
- ❀ Undress your baby down to his nappy; wrap him in a towel on the changing mat next to the bath. Wash his face before he gets in.
- ❀ Take off his nappy last and clean his bottom.
- ❀ Lift your baby into the water with one arm behind his shoulders and neck, holding his outside arm with your hand. Put your other hand under his bottom. Once his bottom is resting on the floor of the bath, you can free that hand for washing.
- ❀ Scoop some water up on to the back of his head to wash his hair. Next, splash water on to his tummy and over his legs. Many babies enjoy this sensation, especially if you sing and chat while you're doing it!
- ❀ When you are both ready, slip your free arm back under his bottom and hold his leg as he will now be slippery; then lift him out on to the towel.
- ❀ Dry your baby well, paying particular attention to skin folds.

Dads are often better at bathing the insecure baby, as their bigger hands feel more supportive. But better still, you could each have a go at co-bathing. Babies love to lie on a parent's chest in the bath and it can be a really special time for you. So make the most of the opportunity to do this during your babymoon, particularly as both parents need to be there (so that whoever is in the bath can pass the baby to the other when they want to get out – it's really difficult to get both yourself and your baby out without help).

How to Change a Nappy

It's safest to change your baby's nappy on a changing mat on the floor. Be aware that when you take off the nappy, your baby will often pee – so have a small cloth ready to fend off the spray from a boy's genitals, and lie a girl on a towel to soak up any spills, otherwise you will find her whole back soaking!

Take off the dirty nappy and wipe your baby's bottom (see p. 193), Then, holding the ankles, lift the bottom into the air and slide a fresh nappy underneath. Bring the nappy up between the legs and fasten tabs.

Nappy contents – what should they look like?

In the first few days after the birth, your baby will pass meconium – a sticky, black tar-like poo, which is difficult to clean, so use a barrier cream in these early days. Occasionally, you may see blood in these early stools, which comes from maternal blood swallowed during delivery.

After the meconium has cleared, breastfed babies will have yellow, sweet-smelling poo, the consistency of scrambled eggs, whereas in formula-fed babies it will be more like an adult's. If your baby's bottom looks at all red, treat it as nappy rash: use a barrier cream and, if possible, let him go without a nappy by lying him on some towels on the floor and letting him have a good kick.

Your baby will wee a lot during the babymoon; maybe as often as twenty to thirty times in twenty-four hours, but you will normally only be aware of this inasmuch as when you change him, the nappy will feel heavier. A paediatrician should be consulted about any baby who is dry for a long time; the postnatal ward or your community midwife will refer you.

Quick meals to sustain you through your babymoon

- ❁ Omelette with asparagus and Gruyère cheese and single cream or Swiss chard and feta
- ❁ Porridge with dates or other dried fruit (this is a great weaning food later on)
- ❁ Wraps filled with just about anything – cold chicken and salad, hummus and red peppers
- ❁ Lentil soup for fibre and iron (stir in ground cumin for delicious flavour); you don't need to pre-soak lentils, just wash them and bring to the boil in stock or water
- ❁ Couscous is very quick to make and great if you feel nauseous; try mixing in chopped fresh mint or any other herbs once cooked
- ❁ Smoothies are good for protein and calcium if you make them with yoghurt; try banana and melon

Bringing Up Wind

If your baby seems to need to bring up wind, there are two ways of doing this:

You can sit him upright on your lap with your hand under his chin, keeping his back as straight as possible. Your baby will probably be leaning forward slightly and you can pat his back quite firmly.

Alternatively, put a good absorbent towel over your shoulder, reaching well down your back, then prop the baby over your shoulder, so he's upright, his chin resting on your shoulder and his tummy stretched out full length against your chest. Now stroke his back and sides firmly and slowly upwards towards his neck several times. Quite firm pressure is needed (a bit like stroking a cat really hard, backwards!).

Most babies bring up small amounts of milk after they have fed – this is known as possetting. Often, this can smell curdled, as it will have been in contact with the stomach's digestive juices. Sometimes, your baby possets as he lets out air trapped in his stomach; so winding can bring up milk too, hence the towel.

Keeping Your Baby At the Right Temperature

Be aware that babies are not very good at maintaining their body temperature. The best way to check your baby's temperature is by feeling his abdomen (his hands and feet may feel cold even when his body is warm). During your babymoon, you will be skin to skin with your baby as much as possible, and you will get used to how he feels, but when you want to get dressed, put him in the same number of layers as you are using yourself.

If your baby is naked, a temperature of less than 29°C (85°F) will mean he is using up energy to keep warm. Obviously, you will not keep your house at that temperature, but it is worth thinking about when you are bathing him, because if the bathroom is chilly, he will cool off very quickly.

Unless your baby is outside a lot (or you have an old, draughty and hard-to-heat house), it is more likely that he will overheat, usually because of too many clothes. Think about how many layers you need and be guided by this – your baby won't need a lot more, unless you are rushing about (which you won't be during your babymooon, will you?).

Even in a hot summer, babies can cope quite well with the heat, as long as they are not too wrapped up. And of course, he needs to be kept out of direct sunlight, as his skin is vulnerable to burning.

A PARENT'S TIP

Mike and I were so scared of bathing our first baby that we put it off for ages. We had left hospital six hours after the birth, just because we wanted to get out of there, so she hadn't had a bath before we left, and after that we put it off because it seemed such a huge hurdle.

The problem was that when Ellie was born, she had passed meconium, so she had greenish poo in her hair for days! Eventually, someone said, 'Aren't you going to clean that out of her hair?' So we had to do it.

But the other problem was that our NCT teacher had said, 'You don't need to use bath products; just use cooled boiled water and cotton wool.' So there we were, trying to clean this stuff out of her hair with cotton wool and water, and we were handling her so gently, it took for ever to get it all out!

Sounds daft, looking back – but at the time, bathing our brand-new baby felt like such a big deal! Of course, with subsequent babies we used soap and other products and were probably much more confident. We learnt that babies really aren't as fragile as you might think, so don't be afraid of handling them!

Sarah, mother of Ellie (aged eight), Thomas (six) and Freya (three)

CHAPTER SEVENTEEN

Helping your baby to adjust to the world

THE CHANGES YOUR BABY HAS gone through in her journey from womb to world are incredibly dramatic, and the first six weeks after birth are a crucial time for her. She is going to need your help to adjust to the real world, and what we will see in this chapter is that most of these adjustments take about six weeks, reinforcing the idea that your babymoon is just what Nature intended.

Firstly, her body now has to adapt to day and night. In the womb, your hormones controlled her diurnal rhythms, and when she is born she loses all sense of day and night. It takes about six weeks for your baby to establish her own internal clock. But you can help the process: when you feed your baby at night, keep lights dim, don't change her nappy unless she's dirty, talk quietly and avoid too much interaction; communicate that this is sleep time.

Secondly, your baby will need lots of sleep during the baby-moon period to let her process all the information she is absorbing from the world around her. At this time, she will sleep far more than at any other age. Unfortunately, however, her sleep will be erratic, not only because of not recognising day and night, but also because she's incapable of sleeping deeply or of soothing herself back to sleep when she wakes. So this may mean periods of being unsettled, especially in the evenings, and again, she is going to need your help to become calm again.

Where Should Your Baby Sleep?

A lot of people tend to view sharing a bed with a baby as either a 'bad thing', or perhaps as a 'consumer choice'. But what both of these viewpoints ignore is what nature really intended: that babies should be in close contact with a trusted adult, probably Mum, until they're capable of fending for themselves. But at the same time, nature did not intend that you become sleep deprived in the process! Pregnancy was actually preparing you for a different sleeping pattern – one that is similar to that of a newborn baby: drifting in and out of sleep, never particularly deeply. As long as you accept this is how nature intends you to sleep and take advantage of your babymoon to doze and rest, you should find you can cope.

Although much of our society believes that it is better for babies to sleep alone, and that separate sleeping encourages independence, there is, in fact, no evidence to suggest that babies who sleep on their own are less dependent on their parents. And it is currently recommended that your baby shares your room for at least the first six months, to lessen the risk of cot death. Evidence also suggests that, provided you do it safely, there is no more risk having the baby in bed with you; and indeed, we now know that bed-sharing helps sustain breastfeeding.

When scientists observe bed-sharing, they notice that mother and baby tune into each other: their cycles of arousal and sleep come together. They also face each other; close enough to inhale each other's CO_2, suggesting that perhaps the mother is stimulating the baby to breathe (perhaps this is why room-sharing is safer for your baby). We don't know how well mothers and babies sleep when sharing the same room (as opposed to the same bed), but it seems likely that your sleep would be less disrupted by having your baby as near to you as possible. You may well wake up more frequently, but less fully.

The main thing about where your baby sleeps is that you are all happy with the arrangements. Discuss what you want to do with your partner, but these are options that you could consider:

- ✿ Both of you share your bed with your baby.
- ✿ Mother and baby sleep together for at least the babymoon, while Dad sleeps separately.
- ✿ Start off each night with your baby in her cot, bringing her into your bed for late-night feeding.
- ✿ Your baby can sleep in a bedside cot (see Resources, p. 232).
- ✿ Baby sleeps in own cot in same room as you.

Safe bed-sharing

- ✿ Don't put your baby to sleep alone in an adult bed.
- ✿ Use as big a bed as possible.
- ✿ Don't sleep with your baby on a couch or water bed, as these surfaces are too soft. Sleeping surfaces should be firm.
- ✿ Be aware of overheating – your baby will need fewer clothes than if she were sleeping alone.
- ✿ Make sure that duvet, pillow or cushions cannot cover your baby's head.
- ✿ You need to make sure your baby can't fall out of bed. You can push your bed against the wall, but it can be difficult ensuring there's no gap between the wall and the bed. Your options are:
  - a guardrail with a plastic mesh, ensuring it's flush against the side of your mattress, so your baby can't slip into a gap
  - using a bedside cot
  - putting your mattress on the floor

Note: all the official guidance says that it's better not to bed-share if:

- either you or your partner smokes
- you have been drinking or taking drugs (this includes prescribed drugs, such as sedatives or strong painkillers)
- you are extremely tired

If one of you smokes, you will be exhaling nasties like carbon monoxide for up to twenty-four hours after smoking, which means your baby is inhaling it while she sleeps. Babies exposed to passive smoking are twice as likely to die of cot death, so avoiding exposure to anyone who smokes is sensible, not just at night-time.

If you have been drinking or taking drugs, you may well be unaware of where your baby is in the bed, and are in danger of smothering her.

The 'extremely tired' guidance is harder to deal with because, of course, as a new mother of a new baby you *will* be very tired! Again, this is about being unaware of where your baby is in the bed – the sleep that comes from deep exhaustion being almost like unconsciousness, which would be dangerous. However, most mothers find that even when tired they are extremely aware of exactly where in the bed their baby is. So on this count, it's a judgment call: if you know that you are so tired that you would sleep through earthquakes and hurricanes, you should put your baby in a cot; but if you are just regular postnatal tired and know that you still have that supersensitive new-mum antenna switched on, your baby should be safe in bed with you.

Soothing Your Baby

Whenever your baby cries during the babymoon, it is going to be challenging for you. You have no baseline. You've never met this baby before, so how can you guess why she is crying – whether her cries are normal or symptomatic of something more sinister? Her cries are not a language where one cry means, 'I'm hungry!' and another means, 'I'm in pain!' You will have to interpret her cries and do something about them, and you will have to do this by context. It will probably take you most of the babymoon period to master this, and you may flounder a bit, initially.

Your baby may not cry much or she may cry a lot. The early days are unpredictable in so many ways. Try to think of this time in terms of seeing your baby's emerging character, as she wakes up to the world about her. She may not yet have formed an opinion of it, and be quite quiet as she absorbs it all, or she may already be unhappy with the place and want to let everyone know her feelings!

In the first few weeks, when she cries, try feeding first. Suckling is comforting, and you cannot overfeed a breastfed baby. If she is opening her mouth and rooting, this is a good indication that she's hungry, so you can begin to look for these cues, and feed her even before she starts crying. If your baby is formula-fed and has fed recently, a dummy can fulfil her desire for comfort through sucking.

If she doesn't appear to be hungry, ask yourself whether she is tired? Babies are not skilled at getting themselves to sleep, and can cry through tiredness. Is she uncomfortable? Check her nappy. Feel her abdomen to find whether she's too cold or hot. Is she in pain? She will probably not stop crying even when you pick her up if she's ill. If you are at all worried, ring your GP.

If you've eliminated all obvious physical discomforts and hunger, then she might just be crying because she is unhappy. Reminders of the womb (see below) often soothe a fractious baby; for her that was how it was to feel safe.

Recreating the womb to soothe your baby

Your baby spent her first nine months being held, rocked and jig-gled around. She could hear your heartbeat and your voice, feel the warmth of your body and the sensation of being held tightly. Therefore, she may be comforted by swaddling, rocking, carrying, by hearing certain sounds and by human contact.

It's best to only use one soothing strategy at a time. This helps you to spot what is or isn't working. Your baby's brain is quite slow compared to yours, so give her time to register what you are doing and to respond. (Think about how long it takes her to smile back at you or imitate you sticking out your tongue, even when she's paying attention.)

She will enjoy hearing your voice as well as listening to rumbling noises like the washing machine, vacuum cleaner or a car engine. These 'white noises' are similar to sounds in the womb. Many babies love music, and we know that they remember the music they heard during pregnancy; so if you had a favourite tune you listened to when you were pregnant, why not try it out again now? If your baby is not one for loud music, try singing lullabies to her. She will probably particularly like it if you hum or sing softly while resting your head against hers.

You can recreate the feeling of restricted space inside the womb by swaddling your baby. Many babies love to be swaddled, while others resist it, but if you persevere, you may find she will settle once she's swaddled. Incidentally, sometimes swaddling is useful just to keep your baby from flailing about, so that you can get through to her with other calming methods – so you could try swaddling, then singing, jiggling or whatever has worked previously.

Holding your naked baby next to your naked body, skin to skin, is soothing. Or your baby may enjoy a simple massage. You don't need to be an expert. Simply watch your baby for cues as to what she likes. Use slow, stroking movements, keeping one hand in contact with her body at all times. You don't need to use any oil, but if you find it helpful, a vegetable oil is probably safest. Don't use aromatherapy oils or scents, as these are too strong for babies.

Some people believe that picking a baby up when she cries, teaches her to cry. However, tiny babies are incapable of comprehending why they might have to wait, and if your baby knows her needs will be met when she cries, she will learn quite simply that

she is loved, that she can influence the world and that her parents are dependable.

Don't worry if your baby seems to need a lot of soothing during these early weeks – it will pass. In the meantime, do whatever you feel is right to comfort her. Keep calm and let your partner take over, if you are feeling annoyed by her crying. Your baby won't cry to 'get at' you or from any other complicated motive, and although it is tempting to project your own feelings on to your baby when interpreting why she's crying, ultimately it will only complicate things.

Cranial osteopathy

You might want to consider cranial osteopathy, if your baby is particularly cranky. A cranial osteopath will look for disturbance in the bones of the skull, and remedy these with gentle massage. The theory is that during labour, the baby's skull is compressed, distorting and overlapping the skull bones. Normally this moulding is reduced in the first few days after birth by crying (which raises intracranial pressure) and by suckling, which also moves the face bones. If the moulding is extreme though, through a very slow, difficult or assisted delivery birth, then the compression stays, making the baby more irritable, perhaps to the extent of giving them a headache. She may cry more and prefer being picked up, as this decreases pressure on the head. It is also suggested that the nerve to the tongue can be affected, so suckling is less effective, and the baby tires before she has had enough milk, so feeding is frequent and erratic.

Cranial osteopathy is also good for babies born very quickly or by Caesarean, who will not have experienced this moulding, which is an important part of her development. Treatments are not available everywhere on the NHS, and in some places, access is limited. Ask your GP to refer you, but you may have to go private. A baby usually needs somewhere between two and six sessions, depending on the severity of the problem.

samantha's recipe for soothing a baby

Someone told me about a 'checklist' for settling babies; this was a godsend for us and we adopted it as soon as we heard about it. Basically, you go through a routine of asking yourself the same questions:

- ❀ Is he hungry?
- ❀ Is he tired?
- ❀ Does he need a new nappy?
- ❀ Does he need a calm time?
- ❀ Does he need a cuddle?
- ❀ Is he too hot?
- ❀ Is he too cold?
- ❀ Is he unwell?

The good thing was that when you got to the end of the list, you could just start again (and again and again . . .) until something worked!

Samantha, mother of Zac (aged three) and Du Rant (one)
(See also p. 220 for Samanatha's story.)

Getting to Know Your Baby

During the early weeks of your babymoon, your baby will not need entertaining. Just processing everything that is happening to her is a challenge: how it feels to breathe, to eat, to defecate, to sleep; what it means when she moves her fingers and toes – all of this is novel, and she doesn't need any more stimulation than this for the first few weeks. So creating a calm environment is really your priority.

As she 'wakes up' to the world – somewhere between three and

six weeks – she may start wanting a bit more input, but just lying with her nappy off, so she can kick, or having a swaying mobile to watch, can be enough to entertain her. If all else fails, watching you will be incredibly interesting!

There is not necessarily an instant falling in love. Many parents take time to love their babies, and the first few weeks can feel odd – as if you are living with a stranger. If you are not aware of this, you could end up feeling guilty, as if there is something wrong with you. But it is perfectly normal to feel like this in the early days. Many parents find they don't really 'fall in love' until the first smile – when their baby starts to interact with them.

What your baby can do

Your baby is born to smile. We know this because blind babies also smile, so it's not just copying. Her earliest, 'reflex' smile may happen in the first few days, usually when she is dropping off to sleep or hears your voice. By four to six weeks you will see a different, more definitely social smile.

Babies are born knowing what a face should look like and prefer these to anything else. Within a few hours of birth, your baby knows your face, telling yours apart from that of another woman with similar features. Soon after birth, you may notice your baby focusing on your face while you are feeding her. Within a few days, she may turn her head towards you when you speak.

Apart from faces, babies are drawn to contrasts. They love looking at stripes and edges, and their eyes will track the outside of objects. This is priming them to learn where an object stops and another begins. They also will track moving objects and understand three dimensions. However, it takes them several months to work out that objects don't just appear and disappear. For a newborn, out of sight is out of mind.

A parent's story

When I had my second son, he fed every one and a half to two hours, day and night. I used to get stressed at night when I was up again feeding, and my husband was able to sleep. It wasn't his fault and I have to stress that he was very supportive of me breastfeeding, but I felt angry that he was getting enough sleep and I wasn't. So I persuaded him that he'd be less disturbed if he slept in the spare room. He did, and for three months it was just Euan and I at night. I'd shut the door and it was like a 'nest', where I felt it was just us, and I could feed him without any of the stress; I remember thinking to myself that I needed to appreciate this time, as it would be over before I knew it.

Euan is now nearly four and I wonder where the time went. Strangely enough, I think I slept better by taking this more positive approach, instead of lying dreading the next feed and feeling bitter at my lack of sleep, and it was better for the relationship with my husband as well. Now I often think back on this special time – a babymoon is exactly what it was.

Joanne, mother of Aidan (aged seven) and Euan (three)

PART FOUR

~

After the Babymoon

Before you know where you are, the babymoon will be over and you will be trying to adapt to life again. I hope that having taken that time to recuperate and having invested in getting to know your baby you will now feel able to meet the challenges ahead. In this section, we shall look briefly at some of the things to think about in the immediate post-babymoon period.

CHAPTER EIGHTEEN

~

Getting back to normal?

How do you decide when the babymoon is over? Well, it is down to you really. You might have felt confident and ready for action long before the six weeks were up, or you may still be struggling to cope some time after this. It can also depend on things like when your partner has to go back to work.

The Six-week Check

The other milestone that may draw a line under your babymoon is the six-week check. After weeks of muddling through, a figure of authority will pronounce you and your baby 'normal', and this can feel a bit like being given the go-ahead for life to go back to normal too – you've had your probation, now you can go back out into the big, wide world!

At the check, your GP will have specific things to discuss and examine. It is worth writing down questions beforehand, as they occur to you, and taking your list with you, as it is sometimes hard to remember everything once you're there.

Your baby's check up

The checks on your baby are similar to those carried out after the birth. His eyes, muscle tone, ears, limbs, heart and lungs are all examined. His weight is checked and his length and head circumference measured, and once again his hips will be looked at for displacement.

This is also a time to discuss any niggling worries, so don't be afraid to ask, no matter how trivial they may seem!

Immunisations will be discussed, but not actually begun. The first immunisation usually happens at three months, but this is a good time to discuss any concerns, as there is not always a doctor available at the time of the vaccination itself.

Your check up

You will be weighed, your blood pressure will be taken, and your breasts might be checked. The doctor will give you a pelvic examination, checking any stitches, and an internal examination to make sure the cervix has closed and the uterus has contracted to its pre-pregnancy size. The doctor will also check that your vagina has regained its muscle tone.

If you have haemorrhoids or varicose veins, these will be examined. If you are feeling very tired, the doctor may want to take a blood sample to check your iron levels. If you were anaemic during pregnancy this will be particularly important.

CONTRACEPTION

Your GP will also want to talk to you about contraception, and may ask if sex feels OK. Many couples will not have attempted it by then, anyway – so don't worry if you don't know the answer to that one! However, the doctor will want to make sure you have contraception in place (even if right now it seems as if you will never have sex again!):

- If you had a diaphragm beforehand, this will need to be refitted, as your size may have changed.
- Some doctors will not want to fit a coil yet in case of introducing infection.
- It's not known whether there are any long-term effects on babies (particularly boys) from exposure to female hormones in the Pill. However, oestrogen does suppress lactation, and so the combined pill would reduce your milk supply; therefore the progesterone-only ('mini') pill is usually offered to breastfeeding mothers.
- Breastfeeding is an effective method of birth control, but only if certain conditions are met, which is rarely the case in the West. Like all contraception, it is not foolproof.

Breastfeeding delays the return of your periods; however, the first time you ovulate after giving birth will be *before* your first period, and you have a 10 per cent risk of falling pregnant if you rely solely on your period returning as a warning that you are fertile, so don't think you are safe just because you have not yet menstruated. However, breastfeeding can also work as a form of contraception which is 98–99 per cent effective (similar to other methods) – this is called LAM (lactational amenorrhoea method). It works if:

- your periods have not returned
- you are breastfeeding your baby on demand, night and day, without using any supplements (usually meaning at least ten short or six long breastfeeds within twenty-four hours with no interval between feeds of more than six hours and no use of dummies)
- your baby is less than six months old

Sex

So what about the big S-E-X question? Maybe *you* have not felt like it; but what is your partner feeling? He may be thinking that he'd like to have sex again, but has no idea how to approach this.

However, it may also be that he feels traumatised by watching the birth, feels tired from the broken nights and is really not that bothered. Either way, it is useful to talk about how you both feel, so it doesn't become a big issue.

As far as you are concerned, it will be at least four weeks before sex after a Caesarean is possible, and this probably feels less uncomfortable than sex after a vaginal delivery. Until menstruation returns, your hormones will not be geared to sex, which means that if you are breastfeeding it may be quite a long time before your body, at least, is thinking about sex.

So for the first few weeks, penetrative sex is not going to be easy. For most couples, it takes much longer for a 'normal' sex life to resume – and perhaps it will never be the same again. This does not mean it will be worse, but it may be different. For a start, there will always be children around who have other ideas! Sex may need to be booked in advance around your baby's resting times (and when they become teenagers, and you're going to bed before them, it becomes yet another issue . . .). Most people find that spontaneity goes out of the window when they become parents. Respect and good communication are vital.

Practically speaking though, if intercourse is uncomfortable right now, you may need to vary positions, slow things down and perhaps use extra lubrication for quite a while, until your hormone levels are back to pre-pregnancy state. Perhaps the answer is to start out with cuddles rather than explicitly trying to have sex, and see what happens. Be patient with each other and talk about it – don't panic, but give yourselves time.

Getting Back Into Shape

You may be raring to go, or you may dread the thought of ever putting one foot in front of the other again, but the sooner you start exercising, even if gently, the sooner your body will get back to somewhere near its pre-pregnancy shape.

The muscles we think of as a six-pack (the rectus abdominis) move apart and can even separate during pregnancy to allow your womb to grow. You must wait until these close again after birth before doing any exercises like crunches. To check if this has happened, lie on your back, put your fingers above your tummy button and crunch up (lift your head and shoulders using your abdominals). You should now be able to feel your abdominal muscles, and if there is a gap down the middle, stick to transversus abdominis muscles exercises (such as in Pilates) and pelvic tilts and floor exercises.

Pelvic tilts

Lie on your back with your knees bent, and as you breathe out, pull your abs in and try to flatten the small of your back down towards the floor and hold.

Transversus abdominis exercise

Kneel on all fours and, with your back flat, pull your tummy in towards your spine. Hold and release.

Pelvic-floor exercises

After carrying your baby and giving birth your pelvic floor is going to need some attention. As soon as you feel able, restart those pelvic-floor exercises we talked about on p. 40. Don't worry if everything feels weak; it will take regular practice before you feel any difference. To check you are doing them right, insert two fingers into your vagina, and tighten round the front, then the back. If you don't feel the grip on your fingers tighten, you are not doing them properly. Sometimes, what you are actually doing is tightening your tummy muscles or holding your breath instead. Imagine trying to stop yourself passing wind and urine at the same time. Once you have isolated the pelvic-floor muscles and are able to be conscious of using them, you should practise two different types of movement: the first is to draw them up quickly, which you would need to do if sneezing to avoid leaking; the second is to draw them up and hold them for several seconds at a time.

Cardiovascular exercise

It's fine to exercise when breastfeeding; there is a myth that it flavours the milk, but no hard evidence. In fact, you probably will want to feed beforehand, so you can feel comfortable and also to avoid being interrupted halfway through.

I would suggest you wear two bras for exercise to avoid any bouncing! You might want to start by taking some brisk walks pushing your baby in a pushchair or carrying him in a sling; try and walk fast enough to get out of puff. Perhaps you could go for power walks with other new mothers?

If you are thinking of resistance training (i.e. using weights), bear in mind that even though you are no longer producing relaxin (see p. 35), it takes about five months for its effects to wear off, so you'll need to take care not to damage your ligaments and joints for some time to come.

It's best to get a specific exercise plan worked out for you by someone who knows about postnatal exercise.

Getting Into a Routine

Many new mothers worry about getting their baby into a routine. But before this becomes a source of anxiety for you, consider exactly what it means. Does it mean doing things by the clock? Or does it mean having a predictable pattern to the day?

Perhaps the place to start is with you. Are you already a routine person? Do you watch the clock? Do you have a list of things you want to do and tick them off as they are dealt with? Or do you take each day as it comes? Both approaches have something to recommend them, and in fact both will end up in the same place, with things getting done. It's just that each way represents a different outlook on life.

When your baby arrives, there is another human being to consider, who perhaps has his own preferred approach to the day. He is unlikely to want to clock watch, but he may actually be happy to fall into a predictable pattern. On the other hand, he may struggle with this; he may find the world a confusing, frightening place, and want to be held, carried and fed constantly, until he gets used to it all.

If you and your baby have wildly different needs, you'll have to negotiate, but wait until your babymoon is over to do this. The main thing to bear in mind is that how your pattern evolves must be something that you both agree on; otherwise one person is going to be unhappy.

For instance it's possible to feed in a routine, and this is probably going to be desirable later on, when your baby is old enough to feed with the family. You won't want to be supplying meals to everyone whenever they fancy it; you will probably want to have at least three meals a day at roughly the same sort of time. However in your baby's first six weeks of life, he needs to feed a lot. His tummy is small and will need to be topped up frequently; he is not particularly skilled at extracting milk quickly from the breast or bottle, so feeding will take him some time. As we saw on p. 170, thanks to prolactin, your body will make exactly the right amount of milk for your baby, if you let him feed when he asks. If you try to impose a feeding schedule, your body will produce the amount of milk *you* tell it to, which may not be the same. Only your baby knows how hungry he is, and how much breast milk he needs. Finally, your baby needs to put on weight – he will double his weight in the first few months of life – never again will he need to grow so quickly. If you had to double your weight in six months, what would you do? Eat often and for long periods!

However, by six weeks, many women find that a pattern is

beginning to emerge, which makes sense as this is about the time your baby's diurnal rhythms are maturing. If you are breastfeeding, your milk supply should be well established by six weeks. If no pattern has emerged and you are feeling the need to get some control over your life, it may be time to start negotiations.

Firstly, keep a diary for a couple of days. Write down what happens and when, and try to see if there is any sort of pattern that you could build on. You can try gradually to extend spaces between feeds, and perhaps also keep your baby awake for longer during a feed so he will take more. Perhaps you would like him to feed a little longer in the afternoon and early evening, so he may go longer between feeds at night. If he is a very sucky baby, you might want to introduce a dummy or let him suck his fingers or thumb.

The important thing to note with breastfeeding is that the pattern has to suit you and your baby, as your milk supply and his appetite are unique to the pair of you. Biologically, it is not possible to say that all babies can feed at 10 a.m., 2 p.m. and 6 p.m., or whatever times you want to impose. Each baby could feed at regular intervals, but how long these intervals will be, and how long each feed will take are not things that can be set in stone.

If you try to impose an arbitrary time on feeding, you will either diminish your milk supply or you will have a baby that does not get enough hindmilk (see p. 172) and who then wants to feed more frequently.

While daytime feeding routines are something that you might work towards eventually, you may be quite keen to have a routine at night sooner, rather than later; by this I mean longer stretches of time asleep, with as few disruptions as possible! Research has found that there are two things you can do to help your baby sleep longer at night: one is to emphasise the difference between day and night (see p. 199); the other is to establish a bedtime routine, the aim here being to help your baby fall asleep on his own in the evenings. Bedtime routines can also be helpful if your baby is fretful in the evenings; a predictable pattern may be soothing. You can also try to pre-empt that crying time by settling him to sleep before it starts.

What you do is down to you, but the sorts of things you might choose are:

- a warm bath – with you or on his own
- a little song (which could later turn into story time)
- a milky drink (breast or bottle)
- cuddles and kisses
- laying your baby down in the cot with some soothing words

You will also eventually want to establish a pattern of daytime naps, so that your baby has definite times for being asleep and being awake, rather than drifting between states as he did in the babymoon; these could evolve alongside the bedtime routines, perhaps with some different cues, so that he knows it is not 'bedtime' – things like leaving the curtains open, playing a soothing tape, leaving a few toys or teddies to play with in the cot.

As your baby gets older, you might find it fun to start living your life to a predictable routine – swimming on Mondays, going to the park on Tuesdays, postnatal group on Wednesdays, etc. Or perhaps predictability will bore you to tears, and you and your baby will treat each day as it comes, deciding on the spur of the moment to go to the zoo or take a train ride. But whatever you choose, and however you live your life, make sure it is how you want to live, and not based on what someone else is telling you to do!

A parent's story

When Zac was about three weeks old, I started to 'come back to life', and would venture out to see friends and family. At six weeks, I noticed that Zac started to get tired at 7.30 p.m. every evening and I thought, let's have a go at a routine. So I started to settle him in his Moses basket and after three nights of persevering with a screaming baby, Zac started to self-settle. What a breakthrough it was; Jaco and I could now spend evenings together – something that I'd thought would be a thing of the past.

Zac was still waking three times a night, but it was fantastic to have a few precious hours to myself to allow me to recharge (oh and to have a bath on my own in peace and quiet!).

By the time Zac was eight weeks old, we had a night-time routine, and I knew – having spoken to other new mums – that I was extremely lucky. My days were spent thoroughly enjoying my time with Zac and showing him off to my friends and family. In the evenings, I could spend time with Jaco. I felt overjoyed about how complete my life was.

Nothing could have prepared me for what the first two months bring, but they were so special and flew by so quickly. I am a little disappointed they have now become a memory (albeit blurred) as I'll never have those times again. Looking back, I really did enjoy them (amid all the sleep deprivation, guilt and worry), and I will treasure the experience for ever.

Samantha, mother of Zac (aged three) and Du Rant (one)
(See also Samantha's tips for soothing your baby, p. 206.)

CHAPTER NINETEEN

~

Celebrating your baby's arrival

N OW THAT YOUR BABYMOON is over, it is time to introduce your baby to the wider world. Probably she is now alert and interested, and seems ready for action. So how about a formal celebration?

Naming Ceremonies

Traditionally, children were welcomed to the world through baptism, which is when they would also receive their name. They would be given godparents as well, whose role could be quite onerous; they were expected to be part of the child's moral upbringing, as well as being willing to step into the breach if something happened to the parents.

You have probably already decided on the name of your child; indeed with most parents now able to discover the sex of their baby in the womb, often the name is decided well before the baby actually arrives. However, you could feel differently once you actually see your baby. Is that Scarlett actually going to be a Melanie?

You don't need to register your baby's birth officially (and therefore decide on her name) straight away, so if it feels right, you could even spend the entire babymoon period deciding on the ideal name. (That's if you live in England or Wales, where you have up to forty-two days to register; in Scotland, you do need to register your baby's birth and name within twenty-one days). Although most people will have chosen a name long before this, a naming celebration can be a reaffirmation of their choice, as well as an opportunity to cement bonds by choosing godparents (or their equivalent). It is also a chance to welcome your baby to the world officially and introduce her to lots of people, as well as a perfect excuse for a small party!

The ceremony does not have to be religious, unless you want it to be. Have a look at the types of civil ceremony on offer in the Resources section (see p. 233). Or you could create your own ceremony.

What's in a name?

In some cultures, a name is seen as so powerful that children are given temporary or 'milk' names until they are old enough to have their real name revealed. Many cultures believe that the child's name embodies her soul. We also have fairy stories in our own culture which reflect the power of names – think of the story of Rumpelstiltskin, for instance.

One study found that girls who were given names rated as highly feminine grew up to be more than averagely feminine adults. Of course, what we don't know here is whether the girls were influenced by the way in which people reacted to their names or whether it was the names themselves that made them feel and act more feminine. But you might just want to pause before you call your daughter Flower or Petal.

If you have not yet chosen your baby's name, here are some things to consider:

- ✿ Try saying the whole name out loud. Something that looks good on paper is not so good if you stumble over it when you speak.
- ✿ Consider what it might be shortened to and any nicknames your child might end up with. And watch those initials too (think of poor old Val Doonican).
- ✿ Your child might not thank you for choosing the wacky or unusual (not even celebrities' children are immune – Zowie Bowie now prefers to be known as Duncan).
- ✿ Having said that, avoid going with the herd. Do you really want your child to be one of five Katies, forever known as Katie B. or Katie D.? And what's highly popular now can also date you: how old do you think someone called Betty might be? And think of all those Kylies in twenty years' time. (Or, worse still, the Lalas, named after a Teletubby!)
- ✿ You might think it safe and traditional to give your baby the same name as you, but it can cause confusion. I have the same initial as my son and I am forever opening his post in error.

A personalised naming ceremony

You might like to choose some favourite poems and ask friends to read them out, select appropriate music or, perhaps, make some vows about how you would like to parent.

Here are some ideas you might like to incorporate:

- ✿ Many traditions from our early culture (e.g. Roman and Celtic) had the mother touch the baby to the ground (Mother Earth), then had the father raise the baby in his arms to face the sun (Father Sun).
- ✿ Another tradition involves holding the baby up and facing her towards the north, south, east and west, then telling these four corners of the world the baby's name and asking for the Earth's blessing.

✿ You could plant a tree in your baby's name, which is symbolic of a long and fruitful life. Perhaps choose a tree to represent something in particular: the oak was revered by the Druids and the Vikings and is seen as the source of many fertility rituals; ash is thought to have healing properties; and in Switzerland, apple trees are for girls and nut trees for boys. Some parents bury the placenta beneath the roots of their tree as it is planted to nourish it.

Recipe for a lifetime of memories . . .

You might like to think about starting a little keepsake box for your baby containing special items to remind you of her early days. When she is older, she will love to share it with you. Things you could keep include:

✿ her hospital wrist band (if she was born in hospital)
✿ the first outfit she wore
✿ a lock of hair
✿ her first tooth
✿ her first pair of shoes
✿ a flower from the first congratulatory bouquet you received
✿ a congratulations card
✿ her birth announcement card.

Choosing godparents or mentors

If you are going to ask someone to be a godparent, consider first what you are asking him or her to do. Is it just about remembering your baby's birthday or do you want this person to be involved in some way in your baby's upbringing? Perhaps rather than thinking of them in terms of spiritual advisors, they could instead be mentors – people your child could call on when they have issues they'd prefer to discuss with someone other than their parents. If this is the role you have in mind, think carefully about who you choose, discuss it with your friend, and be prepared for them to decline if they feel this task is too much.

Other Ways to Welcome Your Baby to the World

If the idea of a big celebration fills you with horror, maybe you could just have a small outing yourselves; choose somewhere special and take lots of photos! Or there are other ways in which you might mark your baby's arrival:

❀ Commission an artistic diagram of your baby's family tree.
❀ Collect together copies of all of the newspapers printed on the day she was born.
❀ Begin a photographic record: take a photo at the same time each week or each month, in roughly the same place, to mark how your baby is growing.
❀ Get a horoscope done: Western or Chinese or both.

But however you decide to mark your baby's entry into the world, make that day a unique and special one for all of you.

So your babymoon is over, and you should, hopefully, have accumulated some precious memories to treasure throughout your child's life. Perhaps by now you realise how quickly your baby changes, and how events that seemed endless at one point are over before you have time to take stock.

I hope that using this book to guide you through pregnancy, birth and the early weeks has equipped you with strategies that you can use throughout the years to come. The job you are doing – creating and moulding a new person – is so important. So take good care of yourself – you and your baby deserve it.

A parent's story

Ina May Gaskin, American home-birth pioneer, talks about women needing to spend hours watching an ant crawl across the floor. The idea is that we all move too fast, but for birth, you need to tune in to another frequency – the slow and primal frequency at which your baby is living and growing inside.

My version of this was watching the wind blow through the trees. I used to be a very high-paced and multi-tasking working woman. However, I learnt to sit and look out the window at one leaf for an hour or more. I'd sit there and I'd breathe. The wind through the branches would be *my* breath, and it slowed me way down. My husband would come home amazed that the woman he'd married was capable of such stillness. But it was a rhythm that changed me on a cellular level, that helped me immensely through my labour and, of course, during my babymoon, and that is with me still.

Sue, mother of Zen (aged seven months)

Resources

Introduction: The Babymoon Concept

To find out more about parenting practices in different cultures, read:
Deborah Jackson, *Baby Wisdom: The World's Best-kept Secrets for the First Year of Parenting* (Hodder & Stoughton Ltd, 2002).

Part One: Pregnancy: A Time to Prepare

For a comprehensive reference book to dip in and out of on the topic of pregnancy and birth, see:

Anna McGrail and Daphne Metland, *Expecting: Everything you need to know about pregnancy, labour and birth* (Virago Press Ltd, 2004).

Chapter One: Yes, You Are Going to Be a Mother!

For some great maternity clothes see:
www.babeswithbabies.com
www.bloomingmarvellous.co.uk
www.maternityexchange.co.uk

For good-quality maternity and nursing bras, look at www.nctms.co.uk. If you want something a bit different, glamorous and sexy, check out the amazing range at www.hotmilklingerie.com.

Chapter Two: Eating for Two?

Visit www.eatwell.gov.uk/agesandstages/pregnancy/ for more information about diet in pregnancy.

Chapter Three: Keeping in Shape

www.pilates.co.uk/Pilates-And-Pregnancy.htm
www.activebirthcentre.com (for yoga classes)
www.postnatalexercise.co.uk

Chapter Four: Chilling Out

Some excellent CDs for relaxation, which are particularly designed for pregnancy and birth, can be found at www.natalhypnotherapy.co.uk.

The Dream Genii pregnancy support pillow is available from www.nctms.co.uk; also useful afterwards for breastfeeding or for helping your baby to sit up.

A new product on the market can help you sleep, day or night. The NightWave Sleep Assistant projects a soft blue light into your bedroom which uses guided relaxation to synchronise your breathing into the right rhythm for sleep. Because it is silent, you can switch it on in the middle of the night without waking your partner; visit www.nightwave.co.uk.

To see what new parents talk about and what they are experiencing, here are some useful chat rooms:
Kelly Mom http://forum.kellymom.net/
NCT virtual coffee morning, www.nct.org.uk/info-centre/egroups or join up at http://health.groups.yahoo.com/group/nct-coffee/

Babycentre is a commercial website, but it is a good source of information, and you can join a bulletin board of mums due in the same month as you and share concerns:
http://www.babycentre.co.uk/community/birthclubs/

For information on mindfulness:
http://www.mindfulnessforhealth.co.uk/courses.html

Chapter Five: Practical Preparation (Or Retail Therapy, To You and Me!)

Get baby nighties at www.buyorganics.co.uk/organic/Newborn-Nightgown(197).aspx.

For slings, have a look at http://betterbabysling.co.uk/; or, as an alternative, there is the Wilkinet, which looks complicated, but once you get the hang of it is very comfy (however you can't breastfeed in it): www.nctshop.co.uk.

The best cot I have seen is the arm's reach co-sleeper, which also converts into a changing table, travel cot and play pen, and all folds neatly away in a bag. It's suitable for premature babies, twins and children up to toddling. It also looks great! Have a look at it on www.sierradistribution.co.uk. The NCT shop also stocks it (www.nctshop.co.uk).

Several companies run first-aid courses, geared particularly to helping babies and young children:
www.theparentcompany.co.uk/index.html
www.safeandsound.uk.net in England and
http://resusfirstaid.co.uk/courses/child_baby_first_aid_training.php in Scotland
St John's Ambulance also run courses particularly for parents of young children: www.sja.org.uk.

Really fab changing bags from www.storksak.co.uk. They also have clips to attach them on to the pushchair.

Chapter Six: Preparing to Become a Family

CenterParcs is a good option for a break at this stage: www.centerparcs.co.uk. They have comfortable accommodation, great spa facilities, and lots of things to do if you are feeling energetic. You can also check out how great they are for families in years to come!

For something more exotic, but still close to home, look at www.kclub.com.

Statistics about changing family structure came from the Millennium Cohort Study at www.oneplusone.org.uk; this is a useful resource for problems with relationships.

NCT may have a babysitting circle in your area or you could form one from your antenatal classes. Ring 0300 33 00 770 for your local branch (9 a.m.–5 p.m., Monday–Thursday; 9 a.m.–4 p.m. on Friday; or visit http://www.nct.org.uk).

Chapter Eight: Thinking About the Birth You Want

NCT antenatal classes: 0300 33 00 770 (9 a.m.–5 p.m., Monday–Thursday; 9 a.m.–4 p.m. on Friday; or visit http://www.nct.org.uk).

Active Birth classes: 020 7482 5554; or visit www.activebirthcentre.com.
For your nearest teacher outside London and/or the UK: http://www.activebirthcentre.com/pb/cat_teachersmap.shtml.

Natal hypnotherapy classes: www.natalhypnotherapy.co.uk
http://www.stressfree.com.au/hypnosisforchild.html (Australia)

Chapter Nine: What Actually Happens During Birth – and How to Cope

For hiring pools for water births, visit www.thegoodbirth.co.uk.

For more on acupuncture:
http://www.acupuncture.org.uk

Chapter Ten: Influencing Your Birth Experience

For more information about small birthing units and other options, check out www.birthchoiceuk.com. You could also ring the NCT Pregnancy & Birth Line on 0300 330 0772 (10 a.m.–8 p.m., Monday to Friday) for a listening ear.

For home-birth support, visit:
http://www.homebirth.org.uk/homebirthuk
http://www.joyousbirth.info/jbcommunity (Australia)

For practical knickers to hold sanitary towels – the NCT sells some really hideous things which are unbelievably comfortable and practical; they call them stretch briefs and they look as if they are made out of string vests, but they do the job: www.nctshop.co.uk/Stretch-Briefs-3-Pack/productinfo/2015/

Two good books:
Sheila Kitzinger, *Birth Your Way: Choosing Birth at Home Or in a Birth Centre* (Dorling Kindersley Publishers Ltd, 2002)
Nicky Wesson, *Home Birth: A Practical Guide* (Pinter & Martin Ltd, 2006)

Chapter Eleven: 'Are We There Yet?' – How Do You Know You Are in Labour?

The National Institute for Health and Clinical Excellence (NICE) is the independent organisation responsible for providing national guidance on the promotion of good health and the prevention and treatment of ill health: www.nice.org.uk. You can download any of their documentation; see, for instance, http://guidance.nice.org.uk/CG70/NiceGuidance/pdf/English for policy and research on induction of labour.

Chapter Twelve: Coming to Terms With the Birth You Actually Had

The NCT can help put you in touch with other women who have had similar experiences. You can ring the NCT Pregnancy & Birth Line 0300 330 0772 (10 a.m.–8 p.m., Monday to Friday) for a listening ear and to talk through your birth. NCT antenatal teachers are on the end of the phone, and may be able to help you understand some of the things that you experienced.

You might want to visit www.birthtraumaassociation.org.uk/, which is an organisation set up to support those traumatised by birth.

Chapter Thirteen: Things Will Never Be the Same Again . . .

Have a look at www.lovefilm.com and sort out a rental list for when the baby has arrived.

Chapter Fourteen: Getting Your Babymoon Off to a Brilliant Start With Breastfeeding

NCT breastfeeding counsellors are mothers who have breastfed their own babies and also gone through an extensive training. The NCT breastfeeding line is open 8 a.m.–10 p.m. on 0300 330 0771.

La Leche League is an international organisation of volunteers who have also breastfed their own babies and been trained to offer support. Go to www.llli.org and type in your country.

Chapter Fifteen: Taking Care of Yourself

As mentioned above, for practical knickers to hold sanitary towels, see www.nctshop.co.uk/Stretch-Briefs-3-Pack/productinfo/2015/. The NCT also hires out special 'valley cushions' which are comforting to sit on with a damaged perineum – see www.nct.org.uk or ring 0300 33 00 770.

The National Institute for Health and Clinical Excellence (NICE) is the independent organisation responsible for providing national guidance on the promotion of good health and the prevention and treatment of ill health: www.nice.org.uk. You can download any of their documentation; see, for instance, http://www.nice.org.uk/Guidance/CG37 for postnatal care.

For postnatal depression, there is a useful and comprehensive leaflet available to download from MIND: www.mind.org.uk.

See also the Association for Post Natal Illness: http://apni.org.

Chapter Seventeen: Helping Your Baby to Adjust to the World

Bedside cots were discussed in Chapter Five; the best one is the arm's reach co-sleeper, which also converts into a changing table, travel cot and play pen, and all folds neatly away in a bag. It's suitable for premature babies, twins and children up to toddling. Visit www.sierradistribution.co.uk. The NCT shop also stocks it: www.nctshop.co.uk.

Chapter Nineteen: Celebrating Your Baby's Arrival

Ideas for civil naming ceremonies are available at
http://www.civilceremonies.co.uk/naming.htm. Your local registry
office may also offer civil naming ceremonies; have a look at
http://www.direct.gov.uk/en/Governmentcitizensandrights/
Registeringlifeevents/Birthandadoptionrecords/Registeringorchanging
abirthrecord/DG_175608.

If you would like something spiritual without being religious, you
could consider the British Humanist Association
www.humanism.org.uk/ceremonies/humanist-namings.

Index

developmental delays 28
diaphragms 213
diaries
  baby 218
  see also journalising
diet 21–33
  babymoon 164–5, 166–7, 173,
    185, 196
  and breastfeeding 185
  carbohydrates 23–4
  drinks 24–5
  fish 27–8, 185
  folic acid 25, 29
  food shopping 33, 71
  foods to avoid in pregnancy
    26
  hospital food 137
  iron 23, 25, 28, 32
  Mediterranean 23
  during pregnancy 21–33
  protein 23
  quality 22
  and recovery after birth 154
  and sleep 54
  snacks 24, 30–1, 38, 71, 124, 126
  see also meals; recipes
discipline 77
diurnal rhythms 199, 218
dizziness 30
domestic work 2
doulas 129, 133
dreams 56
drinks 24–5
  see also alcohol intake
drug-taking 202
due date, going past 141, 145–9
duty doctors 128

ear plugs 136
empowerment 55
endorphins 34, 44, 94, 106, 108,
  116
energy, pre-birth 41–2, 45, 140
engorgement 177, 178

Entonox 117
environment
  birth 120–7
  relaxing 45–6
  for your babymoon 165–6, 186
epidurals 95, 148, 150–1
episiotomy 3, 93, 95, 154, 183
essential oils 12, 53, 184
evolution 89–90
expressing milk 179
extended families 83–5
eyes 13

faces 207
families
  extended families 83–5
  holidays 75–7
  hot topics 77
  new family set-ups 83
  partners 74–5, 78–83
  preparing to become 74–85
  reconstituted 83
family trees 225
fathers *see* partners
fats
  of hindmilk 172
  monounsaturated 23
  omega-3 fatty acids 27, 28, 29,
    31, 32
  saturated 23
  trans 23
  unsaturated 23
feeding
  routines 217–18
  see also breastfeeding
feelings 5, 141, 153
feet 14
finances 77
fish 27–8, 185
fish oil 28
fitness *see* physical exercise
flower remedies 187
fluid loss, after pregnancy 182,
  184

skull, moulding during birth 205
sleep
    baby and 64–5, 77, 85, 199–203,
        218–20
    bedtime routines 218–20
    and breastfeeding 53
    daytime naps 219
    during the babymoon 208
    during pregnancy 52–4
sleeping when your baby sleeps
    85
sleeping masks 136
slings 63–4, 70
'slowing down' 226
smiling 207
smoking 202
smoothies 117, 124, 196
snacks
    babymoon 71
    during pregnancy 24, 30–1
    for labour 124
    for physical exercise 38
    for your partner 126
soothing baby 202–6
spina bifida 29
sterilizers 68
stitches 154, 183–4, 185
stress
    during labour 110, 123
    during pregnancy 43–4, 155
stress hormones 44, 110
stretch marks 12, 13
sun tans 13
swaddling 203, 204
sweating 182
swimming 42
syntocinon 146
syntometrine 133

teeth 12
temperature 68–9, 126–7, 197
TENS (transcutaneous electrical
    nerve stimulation)
        machines 116–17

tests
    antenatal 18–19
    Gutherie test 191
    see also check-ups
thermometers 68–9
Third World 19
thresholds 4
thrush 92, 176–7, 191
tongue tie 180
'topping and tailing' 192–3
touch
    dislike of 134
    see also massage; skin-to-skin
        contact
toxoplasmosis 26
transcutaneous electrical nerve
    stimulation (TENS)
        machines 116–17
transition (labour) 108
transitional periods 4
transverse lie 143
transversus abdominis exercise
    215
travel systems 63
tree planting 224
tummy exercises 34–5, 37, 39, 215
twins 128

umbilical cord
    care 192
    cutting the 130
urticaria, neonatal 190
uterus, contracting back/after
    pains 171, 182

vaginal birth after Caesarean
    (VBAC) 153
vaginal discharge, babies and
    190
vaginal examinations 212
vaginal infections 30
varicose veins 12, 212
vegetarians 28
ventouse delivery 3, 153, 172, 190